Developing Countries and the Doha Development Agenda of the WTO

I0131218

The Doha Development Agenda holds the promise of substantial gains for developing countries. However, the way to realize these gains is far from obvious: the interests of various countries and groups of countries differ widely, and technical complexities have hampered further progress since the very start of the negotiations.

This volume provides an analysis of the main characteristics of the Doha Development Agenda: the trade talks themselves, the increasing complexity of the WTO and its members' conflicting interests, particularly in the area of agricultural protection. The main challenge on the table is to come up with a package deal that serves the interest of developing countries in particular.

The effects of various trade liberalization scenarios are analysed using advanced modelling. Results are presented for various groups of developed and developing countries, including the G-20 and the least-developed countries.

The editors have brought together a group of outstanding experts in the field.

Pitou van Dijck is Associate Professor of Economics at the Centre for Latin American Research and Documentation (CEDLA) in Amsterdam, the Netherlands.

Gerrit Faber is Associate Professor of International Economics at the Utrecht School of Economics (Utrecht University), the Netherlands.

Routledge studies in the modern world economy

Developing Countries and the Doha Development Agenda of the WTO

Edited by
Pitou van Dijck and Gerrit Faber

Routledge
Taylor & Francis Group

LONDON AND NEW YORK

First published 2006
by Routledge
2 Park Square, Milton Park, Abingdon, Oxon OX14 4RN

Simultaneously published in the USA and Canada
by Routledge
711 Third Ave, New York, NY 10017

*Routledge is an imprint of the Taylor & Francis Group,
an informa business*

First issued in paperback 2013

Typeset in Times New Roman by
Newgen Imaging Systems (P) Ltd, Chennai, India

British Library Cataloguing in Publication Data
A catalogue record for this book is available from the British Library

Library of Congress Cataloging in Publication Data
A catalog record for this book has been requested

ISBN13: 978–0–415–39140–5 (hbk)
ISBN13: 978–0–415–64718–2 (pbk)

'Would you tell me, please, which way I ought to go from here?' said Alice.
'That depends a good deal on where you want to get to,' said the Cat.
Alice's Adventures in Wonderland, Lewis Carroll

Contents

Illustrations

Figures

Tables

Box

Contributors

Kym Anderson is Professor of Economics at the University of Adelaide and is currently at the Development Research Group of The World Bank, Washington, DC.

Fabiana D'Atri is at the São Paulo School of Economics.

Pitou van Dijck is Associate Professor of Economics at the Centre for Latin American Research and Documentation (CEDLA), Amsterdam.

Gerrit Faber is Associate Professor of International Economics at the Utrecht School of Economics, Utrecht University.

Joseph Francois is Professor of International Economics at Erasmus University, Rotterdam.

Bernard Hoekman is in the Development Research Group of The World Bank, Washington, DC, and the Groupe d'Economie Mondiale, Sciences Po, Paris.

Michiel Keyzer is Director of the Centre for World Food Studies at the Free University of Amsterdam (SOW-VU) and Professor of Economics at the same university.

Nicola Loffler is Junior Trade Law Advisor at International Lawyers and Economists against Poverty (ILEAP), Toronto.

Julia von Maltzan Pacheco is at the São Paulo School of Economics.

Will Martin is lead economist in the Development Research Group of The World Bank, Washington, DC.

Dominique van der Mensbrugghe is in the Development Prospects Group of The World Bank, Washington, DC.

Constantine Michalopoulos is an independent consultant.

Dominique Njinkeu is Executive Director of International Lawyers and Economists against Poverty (ILEAP), Toronto.

Pierre Sauvé is Research Associate at the International Trade Policy Unit of the London School of Economics.

L. Alan Winters is at The World Bank, Washington, DC, and the University of Sussex.

Jolanda E. Ygosse Battisti is at the São Paulo School of Economics.

Preface

The Doha Development Agenda (DDA) of the World Trade Organization (WTO) is an ambitious multilateral project that aims at integrating developing countries more fully into the world trading system and at contributing to their prospects for development and poverty alleviation. This book does not just take stock of the progress made since November 2001, when the Agenda was adopted, but attempts to delineate the way ahead and indicate what still needs to be done to fulfil the DDA's objectives.

The studies presented in this volume focus on some of the most contentious aspects of the ongoing negotiations: agriculture, services, Special and Differential Treatment for developing countries, and aid for trade. Moreover, they highlight the specific interests of the African and other least-developed countries and of the G-20 as a group of middle-income countries. Both groups of countries represent very different interests while sharing some common objectives as well, and both groups have managed to make their priorities part of an increasingly complicated and multidimensional agenda.

The topics presented in this volume have all been analysed in the context of an ongoing series of international expert meetings held in The Hague, which started right after the launch of the negotiations on the DDA in Doha. So far, six such meetings have taken place, organized by the Centre for Latin American Research and Documentation (CEDLA) in Amsterdam, the Utrecht School of Economics and the Netherlands Institute of International Relations 'Clingendael'. The Ministry of Foreign Affairs and the Ministry of Economic Affairs of the Netherlands have sponsored the project. Its realization has come about through close cooperation among the academics and civil servants involved in the process.

The organization of the entire project, involving expert and public meetings on the DDA, as well as the publication of this volume, could not possibly have been realized without the highly professional support of

Marinella Wallis at CEDLA. Her commitment, professionalism and enthusiasm have contributed greatly to the project, for which we are deeply grateful.

Pitou van Dijck
CEDLA

Gerrit Faber
Utrecht School of Economics

Amsterdam and Utrecht, July 2005

Abbreviations

ACP	African Caribbean and Pacific (group of countries)
AGOA	Africa Growth Opportunity Act
AMS	Aggregate Measure of Support
AoA	Agreement on Agriculture
APEC	Asia Pacific Economic Cooperation
ATPSM	Agricultural Trade Policy Simulation Model
CAFTA	Central American Free Trade Agreement
CAP	Common Agricultural Policy (EU)
CEDLA	Centre for Latin American Research and Documentation
CEPII	Centre d'Etudes Prospectives et d'Informations Internationales
CPI	Consumer Price Index
CU	Customs Union
CUSFTA	Canada–US Free Trade Agreement
DDA	Doha Development Agenda
DDAGTF	Doha Development Agenda Global Trust Fund
DSB	Dispute Settlement Body
DSU	Dispute Settlement Understanding
DWP	Doha Work Programme
EBA	Everything But Arms
EFTA	European Free Trade Area
EU	European Union
FAIR	Federal Agricultural Improvement and Reform (Act)
FAO	Food and Agriculture Organization of the United Nations
FDI	Foreign Direct Investment
FSRIA	Farm Security and Rural Investment Act
FTAA	Free Trade Area of the Americas
GATS	General Agreement on Trade in Services
GATT	General Agreement on Tariffs and Trade
GDP	Gross Domestic Product

GNP-PPP	Gross National Product at Purchasing Power Parity
GSP	General System of Preferences
GTAP	Global Trade Analysis Project
IMF	International Monetary Fund
ITC	International Trade Centre
LDC	Least-Developed Country
MDG	Millennium Development Goals
MENA	Middle East and North Africa
MFN	Most Favoured Nation
NAFTA	North American Free Trade Agreement
NAMA	Non-Agricultural Market Access
NGO	Non-Governmental Organisation
NTB	Non-Tariff Barrier
OECD	Organisation for Economic Cooperation and Development
PSE	Producer Support Estimate
PTA	Preferential Trade Agreement
QR	Quantitative Restriction
SACU	Southern African Customs Union
SDT	Special and Differential Treatment
SPS	Sanitary and Phytosanitary Standards
SSG	Special Safeguard (in AoA)
SSM	Special Safeguard Mechanism
STE	State Trading Enterprise
TBT	Technical Barrier to Trade
TIM	Trade Integration Mechanism (IMF)
TRCB	Trade-Related Capacity Building
TRIMS	Trade-Related Investment Measures
TRIPS	Trade-Related Intellectual Property Rights
TRQ	Tariff Rate Quota
TRTA	Trade-Related Technical Assistance
UN	United Nations
UNCTAD	United Nations Conference on Trade and Development
UNIDO	United Nations Industrial Development Organization
WTO	World Trade Organization

1 The Doha Development Agenda

Ambitions and achievements

Pitou van Dijck and Gerrit Faber

Introduction

Early August 2004, almost one year after the Fifth Ministerial Meeting of the World Trade Organization (WTO) in Cancun ended without substantive agreement, the Doha Work Programme (DWP), which provides the framework modalities for future negotiations, was agreed. The DWP is a crucial step to move the negotiations towards their completion. It is true that the Fourth Ministerial Meeting of Doha in 2001 had launched the ambitious Doha Development Agenda (DDA), but many decisions on the substance of the negotiations were postponed to the Cancun meeting. This included the decision to start negotiations in the areas of investment, competition policy, government procurement, and trade facilitation, the so-called Singapore Issues; in the areas of small economies; on trade, debt, and finance; on trade and transfer of technology; and on the modalities for the negotiations on agriculture.

The Doha Declarations (WTO 2001a) leave no doubt about the ambitions of the members: 'We are determined...to maintain the process of reform and liberalization of trade policies...and pledge to reject the use of protectionism.' These firm words were to end a period in which the gap between the positions of developed and developing countries had widened. Indeed, two years earlier, the debacle of the Third Ministerial Meeting in Seattle had shown that the world trading order was not only threatened by genuine differences of opinion over issues of trade liberalization. The failure of Seattle was in large part due to the rhetoric over labour standards and sanctions without due regard for developing countries' concerns.

Notwithstanding the verbal resolve to make the WTO contribute to development and poverty alleviation, progress so far has been slow. In fact, right before the Ministerial in Cancun, there were no draft agreements among the members on the most salient issues. The joint proposal by the EU and USA on agriculture a few weeks before Cancun was not able to get the negotiations moving again, but triggered a fierce critique of what was to become the G-20, thus clearly demonstrating the gap in ambitions and perspectives between the two major players among the developed countries and a large and diverse group of developing countries in Latin America, Asia, and Africa. It was only in the summer of 2004 that the DWP was finalized and negotiations on the substance, that is, on the extent of the reduction of trade barriers, finally could start. The question is: what package will get the support of all members, in order to complete the DDA?

Rather than providing a blueprint of the 'single undertaking', this volume will delineate the main elements of a development-orientated, trade-related package deal, and formulate the conditions that such a package has to meet in order to be acceptable. By way of introduction to the overall study, this chapter provides an overview of the issues under negotiation and the positions of the main players. The next section shows in what respects this round differs from previous multilateral trade rounds and in what respects the DDA is particularly relevant to developing countries. Subsequently we show in a stylized fashion the significant changes in the world trading system and in particular the rapidly changing position of developing countries. The final section focuses on the main issues on the agenda of the DDA that need to be solved to make the Doha Round a true development round.

The Agenda

Preponderance of development

In the rounds of trade negotiations that took place before the Uruguay Round (1986–94), the roles of developing countries and the attention for their problems were limited. Non-reciprocity, preferential treatment for their exports, and more space for their trade policies were the major elements of the Special and Differential Treatment (SDT) offered to them. At the same time, developing countries did not actively participate in the negotiations on trade liberalization, the core of the General Agreement on Tariffs and Trade (GATT) rounds. This changed somewhat during the Uruguay Round (1986–94), which addressed the issue of market access for export products from developing countries and for exports of services from developed countries to the markets of the South. However, for many developing countries the outcomes of the Uruguay Round had been far less beneficial than expected. The implementation of the agreement on Trade-Related Intellectual Property Rights (TRIPS) appeared very costly, leading to transfers to developed countries' firms (Primo Braga *et al.* 2002). The 'dirty tariffication' of agricultural trade barriers and the backloading of the abolition of quantitative restrictions (QRs) on developing countries' exports of clothing and textiles constituted a further dilution of the benefits of the Uruguay Round for developing countries (Srinivasan 2002).

In Doha, much time and words were devoted to the interests of developing countries.[1] The title of the new round is a tribute to the objective of creating a multilateral trading order in which '...trade can play a major role in the promotion of economic development and the alleviation of poverty' (WTO 2001: Para. 2). Two more declarations complemented the Ministerial Declaration: one on 'the TRIPS Agreement and public health' and one on 'implementation-related issues'. The former was to deal with a conflict that had arisen between developing countries and developed countries over the price of medicines to treat HIV/AIDS and some other tropical diseases. As the declaration puts it: '...the TRIPS Agreement does not and should not prevent members from taking measures to protect public health' (WTO 2001b). The TRIPS Agreement should be interpreted 'in a manner supportive of public health, by promoting both access to existing medicines and research and development into new medicines'. The latter declaration reaffirms earlier agreements and urges members to apply measures in favour of developing countries such as early liberalization of clothing and textiles imports, and support for the implementation of standards.

The DDA has development as its main objective. Given the relatively high rates of growth in large parts of the developing world during recent years, and the increased orientation of the major trading nations towards international markets including markets of developing countries, the latter group of countries has become more active and demanding in international negotiations. This makes the nature of the DDA different as compared to previous rounds of negotiations in several respects.

Up to the Uruguay Round, developed countries exchanged concessions on manufactured products and non-agricultural commodities primarily among themselves. Consequently, barriers to trade in these products have been reduced to very low levels. However, for labour-intensive and temperate zone agricultural products tariffs remained high. Most tariff peaks in developed countries are concentrated in these product groups. Such products constitute a significant share of developing countries' exports.

To be successful, the DDA must contribute to the liberalization of trade in these product groups. However, negotiations on North–South trade will be more difficult than negotiations on trade among developed countries were, as they concern largely inter-industry rather than intra-industry trade. Trade among developed economies is for a large part concentrated in sectors that are characterized by scale economies and product differentiation, and trade liberalization tends to stimulate intra-sectoral specialization.

However, trade liberalization between developing and developed countries tends to stimulate specialization between sectors characterized by a widely different use of factors of production, thus changing the structure of production and the distribution of income over factors of production in the liberalizing economies. Although substantial welfare gains can be reaped at the level of the economy at large, factors of production in declining industries will receive lower rewards or will get out of business. These effects are shown by Anderson *et al.* in Chapter 2 of this volume, Table 2.3, in a scenario of full liberalization of global trade. Those that expect to be negatively affected may attempt to organize coalitions opposing the proposed liberalization measures. The Uruguay Round (1986–94) made a beginning in addressing the difficult task of liberalizing trade between developed and developing countries by integrating rules for the liberalization of trade in textiles and clothing, and by the Agreement on Agriculture (AoA).[2]

The agenda of multilateral trade negotiations has been expanding continuously since the Kennedy Round (1962–67). After tariffs had been lowered substantially and QRs had been largely removed, differences in regulations were becoming major trade barriers. Early examples of agreements on harmonization of regulatory barriers are the codes on standards, subsidies, government procurement, and on civil aircraft, concluded during the Tokyo Round (1973–79). The Uruguay Round concluded with a large number of agreements on harmonization of regulations that deepened previous and introduced new agreements: on Technical Barriers to Trade (TBT), and on the Application of Sanitary and Phytosanitary Standards (SPS). Agreements on services, investment, intellectual property rights, subsidies, and agriculture expanded the area of harmonization of regulation further. For an overview see Faber (2002). The Doha Declarations opened the possibility to take the process a few steps further by addressing the Singapore Issues, further liberalization of services, and by bringing down the trade-distorting effects of agricultural support. However, the limits of regulatory harmonization are becoming apparent. This applies particularly for negotiations between partners that are likely to have widely differing regulatory preferences, as is the case with developing and developed countries. Different levels of welfare are likely to give rise to diverging preferences for policy interventions in areas such as protection of workers, consumers of goods and services, owners of intellectual property rights, and the environment. Forcing developing countries to accept the regulations of the developed world may distort the national development priorities and be counterproductive (Finger and Schuler 2000). For these reasons, progress in regulatory harmonization will be very difficult to achieve. Only where there are sufficient benefits for all WTO members, this seems likely to happen.

Transparency and single undertaking

The deliberations on the DDA show that the negotiations for further trade liberalization are complex and strongly interrelated. The complexity is caused by the diversity of subjects that are on the negotiating table. How should a negotiator make a trade-off between a regulatory 'concession' and a gain in market access? At the same time, it is precisely the broadness of the range of subjects that should facilitate an overall agreement. This overall agreement 'shall be treated as a single undertaking' (WTO 2001a: Para. 47). If member countries could opt out of parts of the overall agreement, the consensus or 'overall balance' (WTO 2001a: Para. 49) that underpins the agreement would crumble, leading to a breakdown in the negotiations. Another complication is the large number of negotiating parties that all have to accept a package, with WTO membership increasing from 124 at the time of conclusion of the Uruguay Round to nearly 150 in 2005. The Doha Declarations promise that the negotiations will be transparent, 'in order to facilitate the effective participation of all' (WTO 2001a: Para. 49, also Para. 10). This is to rule out deal-making among a small number of major players that puts the rest of the membership before a *fait accompli*. Transparency is also an objective of the WTO in its relationships with non-governmental organizations (NGOs). As put in the Marrakesh Agreement: 'The General Council may make appropriate arrangements for consultation and cooperation with non-governmental organizations concerned with matters related to those of the WTO' (GATT 1994: 9, Article V. 2).

Taken together, the increased complexity of substance, expanded membership, and increased openness all contribute to the complexity of consensus making in a 'single undertaking'. Although the time for secret deals among the big players may be past, reaching an agreement among so many partners in dialogue with the outside world will be an even more arduous task than ever before.

The players

Beyond doubt, the complexity of the current round of trade negotiations is largely due to the wide variety in the issues at stake and their inherent technical complexity. At the same time, agenda setting and decision making have been complicated by fundamental shifts in the global economy, which is moving from a system strongly dominated by two major players, the USA and the EU, towards a multipolar system in which new growth poles in the world economy are playing an increasingly significant role, as reflected in their say in trade negotiations.

The emergence of these new centres of gravity among the group of developing countries has resulted in a complicated world-trade network in which several players in Asia, the Americas, and Europe dominate regional as well as inter-regional flows of goods, services, and foreign direct investment (FDI). The new situation is depicted in a stylized fashion in Figure 1.1.

As the figure shows, the USA and the EU are still by far the two largest economic powers in the world economy, as measured according to their gross national product at purchasing power parity (GNP-PPP) and the trade flow between them is yet the largest interregional trade flow in the world economy. At the same time, however, a multipolar economic system is emergent as reflected by the size of the economies in Asia, including the three regional economic superpowers China, Japan, and India, as well as by the size of trade flows between these economies. Moreover, in the Western Hemisphere, Brazil and Mexico are emerging as two regional superpowers with a considerable weight in the world trade system.

Bilateral trade flows are mainly determined by the size of the economies in terms of overall purchasing power, levels of income per capita, access to the domestic markets, the availability of low-cost transportation, and to some extent by the similarity in export supply and import demand of trade partners, as shown by gravity models of international trade. Hence, the emergence of economies and the worldwide process of liberalization have impacted significantly on world trade flows and have resulted in a dynamic and rapidly evolving system of bilateral trade linkages, as illustrated in the figure.

The new role of countries in the South as major exporters and importers in the world trade system is shown in more detail in Tables 1.1 and 1.2. The tables include major regional country groups and the export performance of all developed and developing countries exporting over 20 billion US dollars in 2003. Note that individual EU countries as well as the countries that have become EU members by 1 May 2004 have not been included in this listing of countries. For each region and country, the tables show percentage-wise the destinations of exports and origins of imports, thus facilitating the analysis of the positioning of the major players in international trade and their orientation towards several regions and country groups.

The negotiations on a heterogeneous set of complex issues among nearly 150 players take place in a context in which world markets affect increasingly the levels of welfare and the potential to develop in all countries. To appreciate the rapidly increasing significance and complexity of multilateral negotiations on trade and trade-related matters, we distinguish four trends that have contributed to the diversity and complexity of the current world trade system and with it of the multilateral trade agenda: systemic economic reform and the deepening and broadening of liberalization; worldwide spread of trade-related manufacturing industry and service suppliers; spread of regionalism; stagnation in Africa.

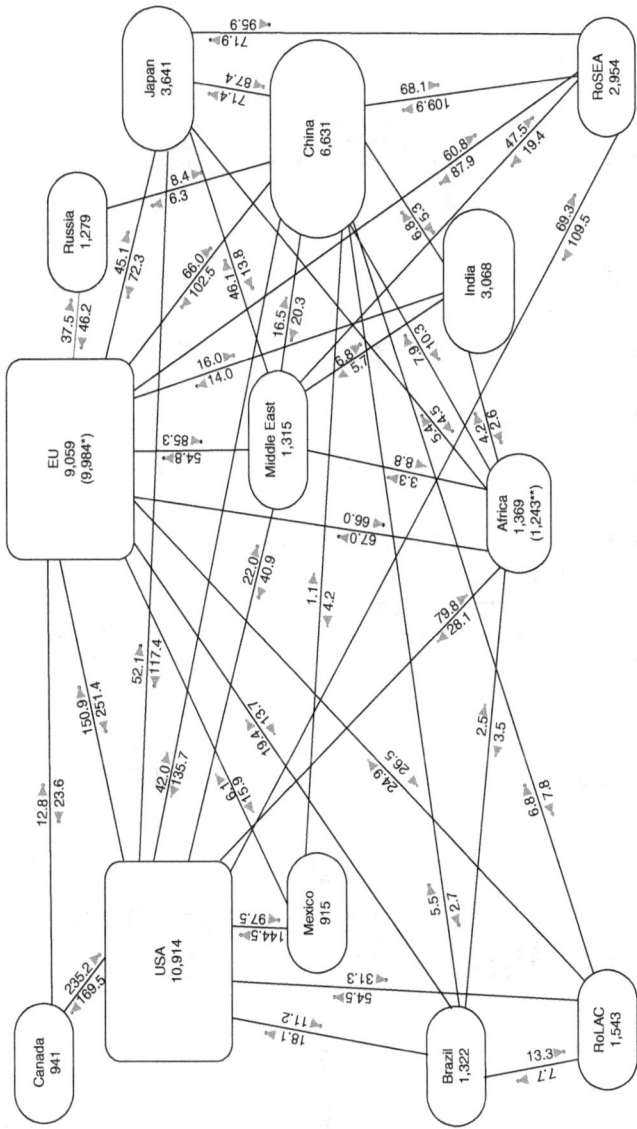

Figure 1.1 Main countries and regions according to GNP-PPP, and main trade flows, in billions of US dollars, 2003.

Source: Data on GNP-PPP taken from The World Bank (2004) *World Development Report 2005: A Better Investment Climate for Everyone*, Washington, DC; export data (DOTS) taken from IMF (2004), *Direction of Trade Statistics, Yearbook 2004*, Washington, DC.

Notes

RoLAC = Rest of Latin America and the Caribbean (Western Hemisphere less Brazil and Mexico); RoSEA = Rest of South-East Asia (Cambodia, Indonesia, Korea, Lao PDR, Malaysia, Philippines, Singapore, Thailand, and Vietnam); * Means including the new members since 1 May 2004; ** Means Sub-Saharan Africa.

Table 1.1 Trade orientation of regions and major trading nations: exports by destination, in percentages, 2003

	Values	Developed countries	Developing countries	Africa	Asia	Europe	Middle East	Western Hemisphere
	Billions of US$							
World	7,492.4	64.6	34.4	1.9	18.5	6.5	3.0	4.6
Developed countries	4,615.9	71.1	28.4	1.8	12.3	6.4	2.8	5.0
Developing countries								
Africa	155.5	68.2	29.8	9.3	12.9	2.4	2.1	3.0
Asia[a]	1,375.1	53.9	45.5	1.7	35.0	2.8	3.5	2.5
Europe	469.4	58.6	40.5	1.0	5.8	28.7	3.6	1.4
Middle East	298.1	49.6	42.5	3.0	28.8	2.8	7.0	1.0
Western Hemisphere	401.2	71.1	25.8	1.1	6.3	1.4	1.4	15.6
EU	2,888.7	77.1	22.1	2.3	5.6	9.3	3.0	1.9
USA	724.0	55.0	45.0	1.1	18.7	1.5	3.0	20.6
	Millions of US$							
China[a]	489,965	67.7	32.1	2.1	19.2	4.2	3.6	3.0
Japan	473,911	44.7	55.3	1.0	46.3	1.5	2.9	3.6
Canada	271,585	94.2	5.7	0.3	3.2	0.4	0.5	1.4
Korea	192,750	43.7	56.2	1.9	42.3	3.3	4.2	4.5
Mexico	164,922	94.0	5.8	0.1	1.4	0.1	0.1	4.1
Singapore	144,121	38.8	60.9	1.1	55.0	1.1	2.0	1.8
Russia	131,454	46.4	53.5	0.7	11.6	37.1	3.3	0.7

Malaysia	104,966	46.0	54.0	0.9	48.0	1.3	2.8	1.0
Switzerland	100,526	77.0	23.0	1.1	9.8	6.0	3.5	2.6
Saudi Arabia	86,219	53.1	46.8	4.2	33.2	1.1	6.9	1.4
Thailand	80,521	51.3	48.4	1.8	40.3	1.3	3.6	1.5
Brazil	78,462	53.5	44.8	3.2	12.5	3.9	4.6	20.6
Australia	70,783	50.0	48.3	2.0	38.8	0.8	5.4	1.3
Norway	68,143	90.0	9.6	0.6	3.9	3.5	0.5	1.1
Indonesia	60,995	51.6	48.4	1.7	40.7	1.4	3.1	1.4
India	60,641	50.4	45.8	4.3	25.4	3.9	9.4	2.8
UAE	49,617	37.9	46.8	3.3	31.4	1.2	11.0	0.1
Turkey	47,255	62.0	33.5	3.2	3.4	14.4	11.8	0.6
Philippines	36,225	54.5	45.5	0.3	43.6	0.5	0.6	0.6
South Africa	35,480	65.6	34.4	14.4	14.6	2.1	2.1	1.2
Israel	31,290	71.0	24.1	1.1	14.0	5.1	0.4	3.5
Iran	31,087	45.6	39.2	1.4	29.3	6.9	1.5	0.1
Venezuela	31,061	61.4	24.0	0.1	2.2	0.3	0.1	21.3
Argentina	29,566	32.8	66.0	3.7	16.9	2.2	4.4	38.8
Nigeria	24,061	67.6	31.3	8.4	15.1	—	—	7.9
Chile	21,464	52.5	41.5	0.4	20.8	1.2	1.0	18.0
Vietnam	20,371	67.2	31.8	0.8	25.3	2.2	3.1	0.5

Source: IMF (2004) *Direction of Trade Statistics, Yearbook 2004*, Washington, DC.

Note

a Calculations involving China exclude trade between China Mainland, China Hong Kong, and China Macao.

Table 1.2 Trade orientation of regions and major trading nations: imports by origin, in percentages, 2003

	Values	Developed countries	Developing countries	Africa	Asia	Europe	Middle East	Western Hemisphere
	Billions of US$							
World	7,745.3	59.2	39.7	2.2	21.5	6.4	3.9	5.6
Developed countries	4,960.9	64.3	35.3	2.4	17.4	6.0	3.3	6.3
Developing countries								
Africa	154.9	57.6	39.5	10.2	15.0	4.0	7.1	3.1
Asia[a]	1,355.8	45.6	51.0	1.7	37.6	2.4	6.9	2.2
Europe	485.1	57.7	41.7	0.9	9.0	28.1	1.9	1.9
Middle East	259.8	54.1	43.1	1.9	22.4	7.3	8.5	3.0
Western Hemisphere	408.9	64.7	33.3	1.2	12.8	1.9	0.7	16.7
EU	2,786.6	73.7	25.8	2.7	9.6	9.2	2.2	2.2
USA	1,305.0	48.0	52.0	2.5	27.0	1.9	3.5	17.1
	Millions of US$							
China[a]	533,796	45.7	49.5	1.7	38.3	3.2	3.3	3.1
Japan	383,025	36.2	63.7	1.7	44.6	1.6	13.4	2.5
Canada	216,266	78.6	20.0	1.3	11.4	0.8	0.9	5.6
Korea	178,824	51.0	49.0	1.3	28.3	2.0	14.9	2.5
Mexico	170,546	80.0	19.7	0.1	13.8	0.8	0.3	4.7
Singapore	127,996	42.7	57.2	0.5	45.8	1.4	8.7	0.9
Russia	56,677	49.0	50.7	1.0	11.6	33.3	0.6	4.1

Malaysia	82,726	48.0	51.7	0.4	47.4	0.6	2.2	1.1
Switzerland	96,344	87.9	12.1	1.3	4.8	3.6	1.4	1.0
Saudi Arabia	53,514	53.3	45.8	3.6	26.8	4.9	5.3	5.2
Thailand	75,809	47.6	50.5	1.2	35.8	1.6	9.9	2.0
Brazil	52,105	56.2	43.4	6.6	13.0	2.6	3.5	17.7
Australia	79,269	58.4	41.2	1.1	36.0	0.6	2.3	1.2
Norway	40,052	79.3	20.7	0.9	9.1	7.5	0.3	2.9
Indonesia	32,544	39.6	59.5	4.6	43.6	1.5	8.1	1.7
India	85,294	34.6	45.4	6.1	23.3	4.6	9.0	2.4
Arab Emirates	55,553	53.1	46.9	1.2	33.8	5.1	5.3	1.4
Turkey	69,458	59.0	39.2	3.0	10.5	16.3	7.7	1.7
Philippines	37,500	51.4	48.6	0.1	38.6	1.5	7.2	1.3
South Africa	34,212	63.2	36.7	4.4	16.3	1.1	11.2	3.7
Israel	34,211	66.3	22.4	1.0	13.0	7.0	0.2	1.2
Iran	30,144	47.9	51.6	0.5	23.5	13.3	10.0	4.4
Venezuela	10,841	54.2	38.9	0.2	5.0	0.8	0.3	32.6
Argentina	13,833	41.4	57.9	0.8	11.0	3.4	0.4	42.3
Nigeria	14,851	52.9	32.0	5.0	18.0	2.4	3.0	3.5
Chile	19,413	35.9	53.0	1.3	12.9	0.8	0.3	37.7
Vietnam	20,371	67.2	31.8	0.8	25.3	2.2	3.1	0.5

Note

a Calculations involving China exclude trade between China Mainland, China Hongkong, and China Macao.

Long-term change

The first worldwide trend affecting significantly the world trading system and particularly the position of developing countries is the liberalization of domestic markets and international transactions, including trade in goods and services, financial transactions, and FDI. In its most dramatic and radical form, this transition has taken place in Eastern Europe and in the former Soviet Union, resulting in the comprehensive transformation of the national economic policy system as well as the regional trade-regulating mechanism of Comecon. A number of these countries have subsequently been integrated into the EU in May 2004, and some more will become members of the EU in the years ahead. The new insertion of these countries in the world economy, which has been locked in by WTO membership of most of them, creates new trade opportunities but also new competition for developing countries, particularly in markets of non-tropical agricultural products, and in a wide range of manufactured goods characterized by the application of mature or standardized technology. China and Vietnam are two more cases in which systemic reform has taken place, contributing not only to overall growth of the domestic economy but also to a radical strengthening of these countries' positions in international trade. Not unlikely, India may be the next in line where systemic transition may contribute to a radical shift in international performance.

Although the process of liberalization in Asia and Latin America has been far less dramatic and comprehensive than was the case in the former socialist regimes, the implications for their insertion in world markets have nevertheless been profound. The newly industrializing Asian countries were among the first to pursue an export-led growth strategy by combining export promotion with partial liberalization and selective opening to FDI. In Latin America, the economic crisis of the early 1980s induced radical change in economic policy along the lines of the Washington Agenda, including substantial tariff liberalization and the abolishment of many non-tariff barriers (NTBs). In the course of the 1980s, many countries in both regions acceded to the General Agreement on Tariffs and Trade (GATT), and subsequently to the WTO, binding their tariff rates at levels much higher than applied rates. Moreover, unilateral liberalization measures have been locked in by preferential trade agreements (PTAs).

The second of these trends is the worldwide spread of industries and service providers producing for international markets, thus transforming radically the traditional division of labour between developed and developing countries, and by consequence international trade flows. Most notably from the 1970s onwards, an increasing number of countries in the Pacific Rim as well as some countries in Latin America, have started to penetrate world markets in a broadening range of labour-intensive manufactured products or goods produced with a standardized 'mature' technology. China in particular has become a new motor in the world economy, stimulating trade flows with countries in all regions of the world. As a consequence North–South trade has become more diverse, and both North–South and South–South trade have been strongly dynamized, contributing more significantly to world trade than in earlier decades. Moreover, a growing number of developing countries are involved in the international supply of services by means of cross-border trade and outsourcing-related activities, and through the international movement of natural persons.

The third trend is the growing role of PTAs the world all over. While the external trade policy of the EU has traditionally been based on a regional and a multilateral pillar, the USA has more recently engaged itself in such a dual approach. Multilateralism, not regionalism, used to be the approach of choice for the USA up to the formation of the Canada–US Free Trade Agreement (CUSFTA) in 1989. Since then, the USA has pursued this new strategy vigorously towards Latin America and some countries in the Pacific Rim. The new approach enables the USA to serve its priorities by negotiating in an interactive way at the regional and multilateral levels. Reluctantly and at a more limited scale, Japan has diversified its strategy as well.

While Latin America and Africa were involved in the establishment of a large number of PTAs already in the 1960s, we may now notice a new momentum in regionalism in all developing regions including Asia. Modern PTAs tend to include a broad range of trade-related issues such as competition policy, investment regulation, and government procurement. This makes strict application of GATT Article XXIV, Territorial Application – Frontier Traffic – Customs Unions, and Free-Trade Areas, all the more urgent. More generally, this trend could contribute to the need for a comprehensive regulation of such trade-related issues at the multilateral level to avoid regional rather than multilateral rules becoming predominant in the world trading system.

Finally an alarming trend, related to the marginalization of Sub-Saharan Africa in the world economy. Over the years 1990–2003, average annual population growth (2.5 per cent) almost equalled growth of GDP (2.7 per cent). The share of Sub-Saharan Africa in world trade has fallen to an all-time low of 1.5 per cent. The region is still highly dependent on commodity exports, despite the various non-reciprocal preferential systems and other initiatives to stimulate non-traditional exports. Although the region is a marginal player in the world economy and in the world trading system, it has managed to create a critical position in the negotiations on the DDA: the potential impact of trade liberalization on Sub-Saharan Africa will be one of the main benchmarks to assess the developmental nature of the DDA outcome.

Regions and countries

What follows is a brief introduction to the position of the major players and groups of countries in this multipolar, complex world trade system.

Developed countries

The EU is by far the largest trader in the world economy, even when excluding intra-EU trade. By 2003, 61.5 per cent of EU exports and 59.0 per cent of EU imports were intra-EU trade. The strong regional orientation of the EU is also reflected by the size of trade flows between the EU and the ten countries that became members on 1 May 2004, and with the four countries that are on the waiting list for future membership, including Turkey, which has a customs union (CU) arrangement with the EU. Not surprisingly, trade of most of these relatively small economies is strongly orientated towards the EU market, with the share of their exports to the EU ranging between 50 to 75 per cent of their total exports.

When adding to intra-EU trade the values of trade of the EU-15 with the 10 plus 4 countries, the regional orientation of the EU-15 would rise to 69 and 66 per cent of overall EU-15 exports and imports respectively. Not unlikely, trade between the EU-15 and the 10 new EU member countries will develop at a higher than average pace in the years ahead when their integration will deepen. Moreover, Switzerland and Norway are two other significant European trade partners of the EU.

The recent extension of the EU with ten countries and probably four more at a later stage not only has an impact on the overall weight of the EU in world trade and hence on its role in WTO negotiations, but will in all likelihood influence its positioning in the WTO as well. The accession of Poland implies a significant expansion of the agricultural production potential of non-tropical products that compete with North and South American agricultural produce. Accession will certainly require further adjustments of the Common Agricultural Policy (CAP) for budgetary and strategic reasons, but internal decision making will be difficult and time-consuming. Also, accession of several countries with industries using standardized technology may reduce the flexibility of the EU to liberalize its trade regime in some selected 'sensitive' manufacturing sectors in which developing countries increasingly are gaining competitive advantages.

A brief observation on the Russian Federation is in place in this context. Not only does Russia possess a rich and diversified natural resource base, but its broadly developed industrial sector and highly skilled labour force also provide the country with a strong export potential for manufactures in the future. After the breakdown of the command economy system and the

Comecon, manufacturing industry will require major restructuring to face intensified competition in the domestic and foreign markets. Future membership of the WTO will only add to the urgency of a comprehensive modernization programme for its industry.

The trade link between the countries of the EU and the USA has been the largest interregional trade flow in the world economy since the establishment of the European Communities. Notwithstanding longstanding agreement among the two partners on the fundamentals of trade policy, and their adherence to the principle of free trade, continuous frictions have been characteristic of their bilateral trade relationship, and conflicts arose on nearly every category of products that crossed the Northern Atlantic (Rood 2000). Nevertheless, the process of trade liberalization has been pushed through by the combined effort of particularly these two players throughout the GATT era, resulting in very low levels of bound and applied most-favoured nation (MFN) tariff rates for most manufactured goods traded between them.

EU trade with Asia, Africa, and Latin America is limited when compared to intra-Europe and EU–USA flows. Ultimately, overall exports of the EU with developing countries excluding developing Europe amount to 12.8 per cent of total EU exports and 33.3 per cent excluding intra-EU trade. EU imports from developing countries excluding developing Europe amount to 16.6 per cent of total EU imports and 40.5 per cent of EU imports excluding intra-EU trade. Figure 1.2 shows EU trade with various developing regions.

For a long period of time, the EU has stimulated its trade relationship with a large group of countries in Africa, the Caribbean, and the Pacific, referred to as the ACP countries, by establishing non-reciprocal PTAs, which allowed ACP countries to pursue protectionist policies while enjoying preferential access in selective EU markets. Preference erosion and lack of competitiveness have limited the impact of these preferences. The EU's new

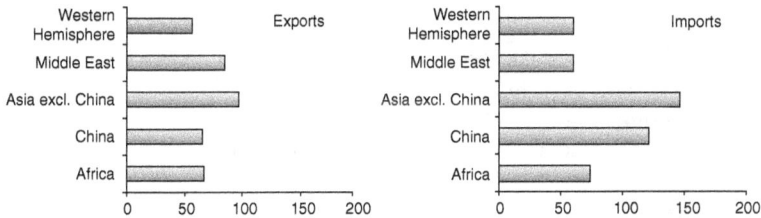

Figure 1.2 Trade of the EU with developing countries, in billions of US dollars, 2003.

Source: IMF (2004) *Direction of Trade Statistics, Yearbook 2004*, Washington, DC.

approach towards PTAs with countries in the South will bring its policy more in line with GATT/WTO rules and will increasingly be founded on the principle of reciprocity in liberalization, as reflected in its new region-wise PTAs with members of the ACP group, and in PTAs with Mexico, Chile, South Africa, and the PTAs that are in the making with Mercosur and the group of countries in the Middle East and North Africa (MENA). Strikingly, the EU has not established any PTA with its dynamic trade partners in Asia, including China (Van Dijck 2000 and 2002a).

As is the case of the EU, the US trade performance is strongly orientated towards the region, and is increasingly being framed in the context of PTAs. The dual US strategy of multilateralism *cum* regionalism was initiated during the Uruguay Round with the establishment of CUSFTA and continued with the establishment of the North American Free Trade Agreement (NAFTA), which is in force since January 1994. Notwithstanding the relative small size of Canada's economy as compared to the EU, US exports to Canada exceed the value of exports to the EU while by now Mexico has become the third largest trade partner of the USA, more significant than China and Japan. A massive inflow of trade-related FDI has contributed to this strong integration in North America. All in all, 36.9 per cent of US exports are orientated to its two NAFTA partners, making NAFTA by far the most important trade partnership for the USA. Unsurprisingly, Canada's and Mexico's orientation towards the USA are extreme: 86.6 per cent of Canada's exports are to the USA and so are 60.6 per cent of its imports. For Mexico, these shares are 87.6 and 61.8 per cent respectively. However, reduction of MFN tariff rates and other measures liberalizing trade such as the new PTAs between the USA and developing countries, including a Free Trade Area of the Americas (FTAA), will erode Mexico's preferential access to the US market significantly.

As a follow-up to the two initiatives related to its neighbours in North America, the USA has started negotiations with countries in Latin America with the exception of Cuba, group-wise as well as individually, to establish a comprehensive PTA in the Americas, the FTAA. PTAs with Chile and countries in Central America (CAFTA) have already been established. The broad agenda of these PTAs includes several of the Singapore Issues, which are strongly contested in the WTO and have been taken off its agenda, at least temporarily, as no explicit consensus could be achieved at the WTO Ministerial of Cancun, which was required to start negotiations on these issues in the DDA.

The new regionalism in US trade policy will not be limited to North and South America, but extended towards the Pacific region and probably Africa. Figures 1.1 and 1.3 show the US orientation towards developing countries and specifically its strong focus on Mexico and South America.

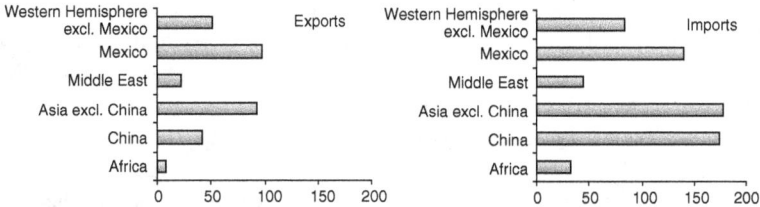

Figure 1.3 Trade of the USA with developing countries, in billions of US dollars, 2003.

Source: IMF (2004) *Direction of Trade Statistics, Yearbook 2004*, Washington, DC.

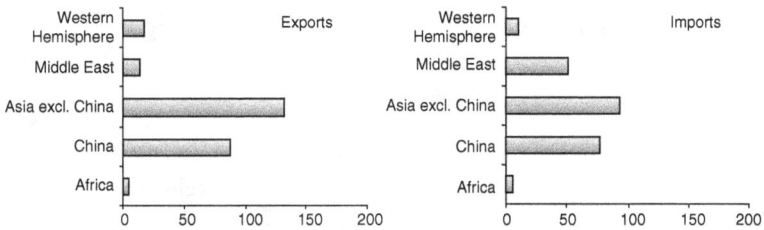

Figure 1.4 Trade of Japan with developing countries, in billions of US dollars, 2003.

Source: IMF (2004) *Direction of Trade Statistics, Yearbook 2004*, Washington, DC.

Long-term stagnation since the early 1990s has caused Japan to lose its dynamizing impact on world trade. This holds not only for Japan's trade with the USA and the EU but also for trade with Latin America, Africa and Asia, except for the booming trade with China. As noted earlier in the case of the EU and the USA, trade has a strong regional component: 46.3 per cent of Japan's exports is orientated towards Asia and 44.6 per cent of Japan's imports originates from Asia, as shown in Figure 1.4. China has become Japan's second export destination with a share of 18.5 per cent, after the USA and before the EU.

Developing countries

China has become the major dynamizing factor in world trade, due to an interaction of strong and sustained overall economic growth of GNP, a large inflow of trade-related FDI and an export-promotion strategy in combination with gradual import liberalization. Concessions made in the accession process towards China's membership of the WTO will further deepen China's integration in international markets and lock in liberalization.

When focusing on the position of China as an engine of growth in world trade, some brief observations are in place on the interaction between China Mainland and China Hong Kong. China's export drive stems particularly from the expansion of trade from China Mainland, which has overtaken the value of exports from China Hong Kong since 1998. A substantial share of exports of both China Mainland and China Hong Kong is essentially intra-China trade: China Hong Kong has become the second largest destination of exports from China Mainland, after the USA and just before the EU, while China Mainland is by far the largest destination of China Hong Kong exports, absorbing 42.6 per cent of its total exports. All in all, by excluding intra-China trade, the value of China's total exports is cut from 372.9 to 261.0 billion US dollars in 1997, and from 664.7 billion to 490.0 billion US dollars in 2003. Although China Hong Kong still is among the largest trading ports in the world, exports from China Hong Kong as well as its imports essentially stagnate when excluding trade with China Mainland. Clearly, the dynamism is concentrated in China Mainland.

China has become a truly global trader, rapidly gaining market shares in a wide range of manufactured products as well as processed food products all over the world. China's main export destinations – excluding intra-China trade – are the Triad powers, the USA, EU, and Japan. At the same time, trade between China and developing countries is buoyant as shown in Figure 1.5. Among its most important trade partners in the South are the traditional tigers in East and Southeast Asia, most notably Korea, Taiwan, Singapore, and Malaysia. Remarkably, while China has generated large trade surpluses with the Triad powers, its trade account is negative with its

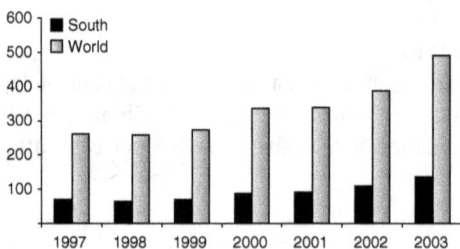

Figure 1.5 Exports of China to the world and the South, in billions of US dollars, 1997–2003.

Source: IMF (2004) *Direction of Trade Statistics, Yearbook 2004*, Washington, DC.

Notes
China includes China Mainland, China Hong Kong, and China Macao. Exports to developing countries including Western Hemisphere, Africa, and Asia and excluding developing Europe. Intra-China trade has been excluded.

Asian trade partners. Apart from the group of Pacific Rim countries, trade has increased rapidly with a large number of countries including Russia, United Arab Emirates, and Mexico, which have become major export destinations. At the import side, Brazil, Argentina, and Chile have developed strong positions in Latin America. In the Middle East, Saudi Arabia and Iran have become major suppliers of imports. In Africa, Nigeria, and South Africa have become major export destinations, while imports are shipped from a wide range of countries in that region. China's broad orientation is also reflected in a low share of regional trade as compared to the Triad Powers – 19.2 per cent of China's exports when excluding intra-China trade.

Apart from China there are six other nations in South and Southeast Asia generating over 50 billion US dollars of exports in 2003 (export values in billions of US dollar in brackets): India (60.6), Korea (192.7), Malaysia (105.0), Singapore (144.1), and Thailand (80.5), as well as Taiwan (not included in IMF 2004). Clearly, countries of the earlier generations of tiger economies are now at a more moderate export growth path than China is, although Korea still shows extremely high export dynamism. Moreover, Vietnam and India are among the new generation of successful export performers in the region.

As compared to earlier decades, comparative advantages of tiger economies have shifted away from labour-intensive and relatively standardized products towards a broader range of products characterized by a wider variety of factor inputs. China's exports to the Triad Powers, and particularly labour-intensive exports such as clothing, replace in part exports by earlier generations of tiger economies, while liberalization of international trade in clothing and textiles, as agreed in the Uruguay Round, facilitates this process. At the same time, new forms of interactions and new trade flows among these countries in Asia are being developed. Tables 1.1 and 1.2 show the generally high contribution of intra-regional trade in many of these Asian countries. Put together, about one-third (34.1 per cent in 1997 and 35.0 per cent in 2003) of developing Asia's exports, excluding intra-China exports, is orientated towards Asia. As a consequence of the relative large size of these trade flows, South–South trade among all developing countries is largely dominated by Asian countries, as shown in Figure 1.6: over 80 per cent of South–South trade is generated by Asian countries as exporters or importers, and about 65 per cent is trade among Asian countries.

Western Hemisphere

Focusing on the position of the Western Hemisphere in the world trading system, we notice wide differences in trade performance and regional orientation between the two largest trading nations in the region, Mexico and Brazil.

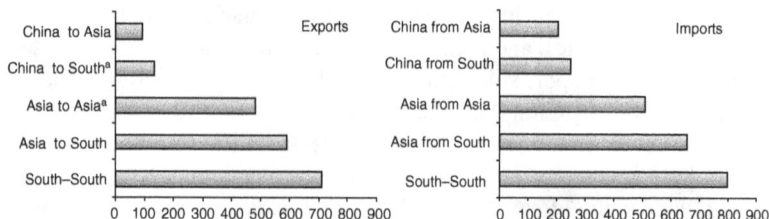

Figure 1.6 Asia in South–South trade, in billions of US dollars, 2003.

Source: IMF (2004) *Direction of Trade Statistics, Yearbook 2004*, Washington, DC.

Notes
Developing countries include Western Hemisphere, Africa, and Asia and excluded, excluding developing Europe. Intra-China trade has been excluded.
a Excluding developing Europe and excluding intra-China trade.

Although the size of Mexico's economy is about 70 per cent of Brazil's GNP at PPP (2003 data), Mexico's exports of 165 billion US dollars exceed by far Brazil's exports of 78 billion US dollars. Put together, the two countries generate 60 per cent of exports and 54 per cent of imports of Latin America and the Caribbean.

Traditionally, Mexico's economy has been linked strongly with the US economy through trade and FDI flows, be it that this was limited in the era of import-substitution policies by high import tariffs, frequent use of NTBs and strict investment regulations. However, integration has progressed rapidly since Mexico's liberalization in the mid-1980s and more specifically as a consequence of NAFTA. Reduction of applied MFN rates in a DDA will result in preference erosion for Mexico. Although Mexico has attempted to diversify its trade and investment position by signing PTAs with the EU and other trade partners in Latin America and Asia, its orientation towards the USA is still extreme, as noted earlier.

Many small economies in Central America and the Caribbean also show a strong trade orientation towards the USA, and this holds to a lesser extent for Colombia and Venezuela. As many of these economies enjoy preferential access to the US economy, they will suffer from preference erosion in case of significant MFN tariff cuts in the WTO. This holds also for the preferences of Caribbean ACP countries in the EU market, be it that the future value of such preferences has already been reduced by WTO rulings on the EU regimes for sugar and bananas.

All the rest of the Western Hemisphere shows a significantly stronger orientation towards the region than Mexico does. However, it is remarkable that notwithstanding a spaghetti bowl of numerous PTAs and bilateral investment treaties among the countries in the region, regional trade in Latin America, both including and excluding Mexico, has not increased but stagnated in absolute terms since 1997, and even declined in relative terms from 29.9 per cent of total exports of countries in the Western Hemisphere excluding Mexico in 1997 to 20.9 per cent in 2003. A similar declining trend is noticeable in the case of Brazil, the great promoter of integration in the region.

As compared to many countries in East and Southeast Asia, the Western Hemisphere does not seem to be strongly orientated towards its own region, as shown also in Tables 1.1 and 1.2. This need not come as a surprise as the export performance of most countries in the Western Hemisphere is strongly dominated by primary products, shipped particularly towards the markets of developed countries, with Mexico being the most significant exception. Moreover, in view of the relatively low applied MFN rates for manufactured products in most countries in the region, the region can no longer be considered inward-orientated as it used to be in the past.

As compared to Mexico, the second largest trading nation of the region, Brazil, shows a more balanced distribution of trade among its partners in the Western Hemisphere, the USA, and the EU. Remarkably, notwithstanding the creation of Mercosur operating *de facto* as a CU, Brazil's trade with Argentina has declined significantly since 1997 (Van Dijck 2002b).

Trade with Asia, and particularly with China, is dynamic, but still rather limited in size. This holds for Brazil and other countries in Latin America such as Argentina and Chile. Rapidly rising demand in China for natural resources for its industry, and for food and food products including soya, is directly stimulating trade between Latin America and China, and contributes indirectly to welfare in the region through an upward impact on commodity prices in international markets. Such an improvement of terms of trade for commodity exporters also contributes to export revenues and producer surplus in other developing regions strongly dependent on commodity exports, such as Africa and the Middle East.

The growing significance of China as an importer of Latin American commodities is also reflected by Brazil's initiatives to strengthen cooperation with China. This would fit in with Brazil's broader policy stance, which goes back already several decades, to promote regional cooperation in order to reduce dependence on the North. Cases in point are Brazil's efforts to create a regionwide PTA in Latin America, its recent initiative to strengthen the functioning of the G-20 in the WTO negotiations, and its initiatives to foster special and preferential bilateral relations with several countries in the South including South Africa and India. The rise of China, however, not only contributes to Brazil's export potential but may also jeopardize Brazil's aspirations of becoming a platform for automobile assembly for the international market.

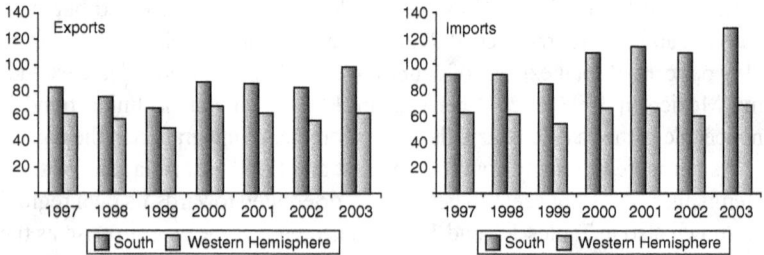

Figure 1.7 The Western Hemisphere in South–South trade, in billions of US dollars, 1997–2003.

Source: IMF (2004) *Direction of Trade Statistics, Yearbook 2004*, Washington, DC.

Note
Developing countries including Western Hemisphere, Africa, and Asia and excluding developing Europe.

Strongly increased openness and new initiatives to strengthen the insertion into international markets contribute to the future role of the Western Hemisphere as another centre of gravity in world trade flows and a dynamizing factor in South–South trade, as illustrated in Figure 1.7. However, the region's overall economic growth and trade performance lacks the sustained dynamism that has been characteristic of East and Southeast Asia.

Africa and the Middle East

Compared to Asia and Latin America, Africa's overall economic growth and growth of international trade are low. Trade of most African countries is strongly orientated towards the markets of developed countries. More specifically, over 40 per cent of Africa's trade is with member countries of the EU. On the basis of former colonial relations, the EU has established a range of PTAs with African countries that are part of the ACP group. These arrangements have given Africa the most privileged position of all on EU markets. Serious doubts have been raised regarding the effectiveness of non-reciprocal preferences, as the share of the ACP countries in EU imports from third countries declined from 8 per cent in 1980 to 3 per cent in 2001. This brought the ACP and the EU to start negotiations on WTO compatible, reciprocal regional partnership agreements within the framework of the Cotonou Agreement. These regional partnership agreements will come into force in 2008. Increased competition in these markets is expected to stimulate sustainable economic growth and the future value of ACP preferences to be eroded by the liberalization of the CAP of the EU. Finally, reduction of export subsidies for agricultural products in the EU may increase prices for food-importing African countries. Hence, the transformation of the PTAs linking African countries with the EU, and the CAP reform required by the DDA, will create major adjustment problems for many African countries.

Apart from the treaties with ACP countries, the EU has established several forms of preferential arrangements with countries in the Maghreb – Algeria, Tunisia, and Morocco – and is still in the process of making special and preferential arrangements with the MENA countries. More recently, a PTA with South Africa has been established.

Concluding remarks

Before presenting the issues under negotiation, some observations are in place pertaining to the findings presented earlier. As shown, market forces and government policies have contributed to a deeper and more diverse integration of developing countries in the world trade system. The wide variation in levels of development among developing countries is reflected in widely different factor availabilities, comparative advantages, and capabilities to compete internationally. The emergence of new centres of gravity has contributed to the opportunity to expand South–South trade. Improved market access in the areas of agricultural goods, manufactures and services, and strict regulations to discipline powerful players, are required to stimulate specialization and trade.

The increased reliance on trade for development has contributed to a more profound interest of developing countries in a broad range of issues in the multilateral trade agenda. As noted earlier, the number of developing countries that has bound tariffs in the GATT/WTO has increased strongly since the early 1980s. Notwithstanding major steps to liberalize their trade regimes, many developing countries still pursue protectionist policies, as reflected by the rates at which import tariffs are bound in the WTO. In most proposals made in the negotiations on the DDA the levels of bound rates – not applied rates – are used for the formulation of concessions. See Table 1.3 for an overview of tariff coverage, and levels of bound and applied rates in developed and developing countries in 2002. For a further analysis of the tariff overhang see Joseph Francois in Chapter 4 of this volume and Table 4.1. For data on applied tariff rates for agricultural products, see Table 2.5.

Moreover, many governments in low-income and small economies are still strongly dependent on import tariff revenues for financing their expenditures. Also, they are still highly dependent on commodity markets for export revenues, which holds particularly for African countries where

Table 1.3 Binding coverage, levels of bound, and applied tariff rates in selected countries, in percentages, 2002

	Binding coverage	Simple average bound rates	Simple average applied rates
Argentina	100.0	31.9	14.2
Bolivia	100.0	40.0	9.4
Chile	100.0	25.1	6.0
Colombia	100.0	42.9	12.3
Mexico	100.0	34.9	18.0
Paraguay	100.0	33.5	12.5
Peru	100.0	13.7	30.1
Uruguay	100.0	31.7	12.8
Venezuela	99.9	36.8	12.7
China	100.0	10.0	12.4
Korea	94.4	16.1	11.6
Singapore	69.2	6.9	0.0
Thailand	74.7	25.7	16.1
Taiwan	100.0	6.1	6.9
EU	100.0	4.1	4.2
USA	100.0	3.6	3.9

Source: WTO (2004), *World Trade Report 2004*, Geneva: World Trade Organization.

manufacturing and the services industry do not yet provide a broad basis for trade. To a lesser extent this holds as well for selected countries in Latin American and Asia. Hence, if the DDA is to serve development, the final outcome of the round must address widely divergent problems developing countries are facing to make trade contribute to development and poverty alleviation, as shown in the following section of this chapter.

Delays and progress: the negotiations

The WTO members agreed to complete the Doha Round by the end of 2004, but it was generally understood that this was an overoptimistic schedule. The positions of the main players appeared to be far apart in a number of important areas. Instead of narrowing the gaps in the negotiating process, wider differences became apparent in crucial areas like agriculture and the Singapore Issues. Between the WTO Ministerials in Doha (2001) and Cancun (2003), the Doha Declarations as such seemed to lose support as 'some country groups began disowning important parts of the Doha Development Agenda' (Das 2004). As a result, the preparations for the Fifth Ministerial Meeting of Cancun were far from complete. Essentially, the meeting was dominated by exchanges of views and coalition formation. Although the members could not agree on the future direction of the negotiations, some important results were to be observed: the EU dropped three of the four Singapore Issues, and there was some flexibility in the positions on agriculture.

Soon after Cancun, the negotiating process was resumed and the willingness to compromise tended to grow with the approaching self-imposed deadline of end July 2004. The DWP has brought agreements in some crucial areas, which may give the negotiations the required direction. Phasing out of export subsidies and lowering of trade barriers in agriculture have become imaginable; a basic understanding has emerged of how to lower tariffs on manufactured products and how to make border formalities less of a trade barrier. Negotiators could now move forward on substantive issues, to be reviewed in the following paragraphs.

Agriculture

The negotiations on the liberalization of world trade in agricultural products constitute the most important section of the DDA for two reasons. First, trade barriers for agricultural products are much higher than for other products: the world average of applied MFN tariffs for agricultural products is 17 per cent, and 9 per cent for manufactures (WTO 2003: 127). For a number of individual products, some countries apply extremely high tariffs. Tariff peaks in agriculture are often concealed by specific tariffs (Acharya and Daly 2004). Moreover, domestic support (subsidies) for agriculture amounted to 227 billion US dollars per year on an average over the period 1995–98, of which 84 per cent was provided by Canada, the EU, Japan, and the USA (Hoekman *et al.* 2004). Second, many developing countries are highly dependent on exports of agricultural products. For example, in 12 least-developed countries (LDCs) agricultural products constitute more than half of total exports (WTO 2003). On the other hand, net food importers among the developing countries stand to lose from trade liberalization, as this will make imports more expensive.[3]

Negotiations on agriculture had already started in 2000, as decided in the Uruguay Round. In Doha, the WTO Ministers repeated that the long-term objective is 'a fair and market-oriented trading system'. The aim of the DDA is: 'substantial improvements in market access; reductions of, with a view to phasing out, all forms of export subsidies; and substantial reductions in trade-distorting domestic support'. In March 2003, the members would have reached an agreement on the modalities for liberalization, which would have enabled the Fifth Ministerial in Cancun to discuss comprehensive draft schedules for liberalization. These deadlines were missed. A few weeks before Cancun, the EU and the USA handed in a framework agreement for modalities, the Joint EC–US Paper on Agriculture, which subsequently served as the basis for the text underlying the negotiations. Shortly before the Fifth Ministerial, the G-20 – a newly formed and diverse coalition of 20 developing countries, 11 of which were members of the Cairns Group – issued a counter-proposal to end all export subsidies, to abolish the Blue Box (subsidies for reducing production), and to lower substantially other forms of income-support as well as import tariffs. Developing countries would retain the opportunity to maintain tariffs and support.

The WTO members discussed all proposals made by the various members. The chairman of the agricultural negotiations produced a new draft for the modalities that was not accepted and the meeting came to an end without an agreement. To a large extent, these revised draft modalities are identical to the EU–USA agreement: a formula approach to tariff reduction that reduces high tariffs more than proportionally; full abolition of export subsidies: 50 per cent of budgetary outlays in five years, the rest in nine years. The Green Box is maintained in the draft. Moreover, the text provides for more gradual implementation and less obligations for developing countries. The main bones of contention were the speed of abolition of the Blue Box, of the export subsidies and obligations for developing countries.

The DWP of August 2004 gave the modalities for the negotiations on the trade liberalization as such. According to plan, the balance of the agreement will only be found at the end of the negotiations and within the overall result of the DDA (WT/L/579, Annex. A, Para. 2). Apparently, WTO members foresaw that some members – among them net-food-importing developing countries – would not find sufficient benefits in the results of the agricultural negotiations as such, and will have to be compensated in other parts of the package. The DWP continues: 'To achieve this balance, the modalities to be developed will need to incorporate operationally effective and meaningful provisions for Special and Differential Treatment for developing countries.'

Trade-distorting domestic support is to be reduced following a harmonizing formula that leads to more reduction by members that provide higher levels of support. In the first year of implementation, the sum of this support will be reduced by at least 20 per cent.[4] Support supplied in the framework of production-limiting and reform programmes, the Blue Box, will remain possible, but will be constrained to a maximum of 5 per cent of the total value of agricultural production during a historical period. The criteria to determine whether support is not or is minimally trade-distorting, that is, whether these measures can be put in the Green Box, will be reviewed.

As to export subsidies, the members agreed to eliminate all forms of export subsidies and to formulate disciplines on measures with equivalent effect such as export credits and food aid. A parallel reduction by all members is an explicit element of the DWP.

With respect to market access, they agreed 'to ensure that a single approach for developed and developing country members meets all the objectives of the Doha Mandate, tariff reductions will be made through a tiered formula that takes into account their different tariff structures'. The formula will have to generate substantial trade expansion. Each member will make a contribution, except LDCs. Higher tariffs will be cut more. However, for Sensitive Products 'flexibilities' will be possible, which means that tariff quotas may not disappear. Still, market access will be improved for these products as well. Developing countries may designate Special Products that will be eligible for more flexible treatment. A Special Safeguard Mechanism will be established for developing countries and no reduction commitments will be demanded from LDCs.

On agriculture the most concrete agreements are on the phasing out of export subsidies and the like, a tiered formula for improving market access, and trade-distorting domestic support. However, there will still be opportunities for member states to limit the lowering of protection for Sensitive and Special Products. The final Doha package will determine the extent of these exceptions, which could limit the value of concessions significantly.

Market access for non-agricultural products

As a result of the first eight rounds of trade negotiations, developed countries diminished their tariffs on manufactured products to an average of less than 4 per cent (Acharya and Daly 2004). However, tariff rates are far above average for sectors such as textiles and clothing, steel, trucks, footwear – to mention a few, for which several developing countries have a comparative advantage and significant export interests. Moreover, there is an anti-processing tendency in the tariff structure of most countries. Developing countries generally have much higher tariffs on non-agricultural products than developed countries have, and in many cases their applied rates are far below the levels at which they have bound their tariffs in earlier WTO Agreements. In addition, many developing countries have only bound part of their tariffs. Hence the significance of the issue of which tariff category – bound or applied – has to be used as a basis for tariff reduction. In Doha, the member countries agreed to reduce or eliminate tariffs, with special attention for high and peak tariffs and tariff escalation. NTBs, particularly on products of export interest to developing countries, were to be addressed as well.

Between Doha (2001) and Cancun (2003), no agreement was reached on a formula for tariff reductions. While developed countries proposed global and substantial reductions, developing countries were more reluctant, particularly as far as their own high tariffs were concerned. They were not prepared to give away concessions as long as negotiations on agriculture did not produce acceptable results.

In the DWP member states agree that a 'non-linear formula on a line-by-line basis' will be used, 'which shall take fully into account the special needs and interests of developing and least-developed country participants…' There will be no *a priori* exclusions of products. Reductions will be made using bound rates, and in case of unbound rates the MFN applied rate will be taken, multiplied by a factor. The text mentions factor two, albeit in brackets. *Non-ad valorem* tariffs will be converted in *ad valorem* duties. Developing countries that have bound less than about one-third of their tariffs will not be required to reduce their tariffs according to the formula, but are expected to bind their tariffs on manufactured products at an average level that is not higher than the average of bound tariffs of all developing countries.[5] For developing countries there is SDT in different aspects, such as length of implementation periods, size of cuts, and the possibility to keep some tariff lines unbound.[6]

The framework agreement on market access for manufactured products lays down some important principles. First, a non-linear formula is to be applied that will bring down high and peak tariffs substantially, which will improve market access for developing countries in developed countries. Second, a very high level of binding will improve the transparency of trade policy of the developing countries concerned. It will depend on the parameters of the formula whether there will be a substantial lowering of the applied tariffs by developing countries as reductions are taken from bound levels. In the course of 2005 it has become clear that some developing countries try to limit their liberalization obligations by adaptation of the formula ('differentiated coefficients'), while others try to retain unbound tariffs for a number of tariff lines.

Market access for services

One of the reasons for the difficult start of the Uruguay Round in 1986 was the wish of some developed countries to start negotiations on the liberalization of services. In Doha, this subject was no longer a bone of contention. During the Uruguay Round a General Agreement on Trade in Services (GATS) was reached, which is primarily a framework for the liberalization of concrete service sectors. Further negotiations started in 1995 and have led to agreements on financial services and on telecom services in 1997. The negotiations restarted in 2000 and were included in the DDA. Negotiations have taken place on a request and offer basis. As a result of this bottom-up approach, the explicit reciprocity that is found in other sectors of the WTO negotiations has been lacking. Governments decide what sectors to liberalize and to what extent. Generally speaking, the commitments under the GATS generally follow at a distance the liberalization that countries introduced earlier.

Members handed in requests and made their offers in March 2003. At the same time, they adopted an agreement on the modalities for further negotiations, which enables them to negotiate bilaterally. Ultimately, the set of bilateral agreements should lead to a multilateral deal that will be part of the final package. The DWP urges members that have not yet submitted their offers to do so as soon as possible. Members promised to strive to make high quality offers, particularly in sectors and modes of supply that are of export interest to developing countries, and not to exclude *a priori* certain sectors. The movement of natural persons is mentioned explicitly in the DWP. This category of service exports is of interest to developing countries, as remittances of workers abroad are a growing source of income.[7]

Although many WTO members have made offers, and an agreement on modalities has been reached, some issues will remain contentious. The temporary movement of workers is one of them. Others are maritime transport and the liberalization of public services.

Special and Differential Treatment and development

SDT and development are included in almost every paragraph of the Doha Declarations and the DWP. Three kinds of SDT can be distinguished: lower levels of obligations, longer time periods for implementation, and technical assistance. Although it is part of every negotiating issue, SDT is also treated as a separate issue. All SDT provisions and 88 agreement-specific proposals on SDT need to be reviewed by the Committee on Trade and Development. This Committee also negotiates on cross-cutting issues that include the principles and objectives of SDT. Members are divided over the question of priority for one of the two approaches. As SDT is an exception to the underlying principle of non-discrimination, basic issues of the world trading order are at stake. It might be argued that a structural exception for developing countries to undertake obligations in the WTO undermines their participation in the negotiating process, and in fact has enabled the liberalization process to pass over the products of special importance to developing countries (Hoekman *et al.* 2002). Trade-Related Technical Assistance (TRTA) is also an important element in assisting poor countries in negotiations and implementation of WTO rules and in adjusting their economies to trade liberalization. The DWP confirms the Doha Declarations and urges members to make further progress in this area.

Trade facilitation

To conform to all official requirements in international transactions may entail high costs in the form of waiting time, documentation, fees, inspection, and testing. As such, this is an NTB to trade. The size of this type of non-transparent barrier is estimated at 2 per cent of the value of trade in the EU before the Single Market programme was introduced, while this percentage was estimated at 5 to 10 per cent in the case of the Asia Pacific Economic Cooperation (APEC) (Francois *et al.* 2002). GATT Article V, Freedom of Transit; Article VIII, Fees and Formalities Connected with Importation and Exportation; and Article X, Publication and Administration of Trade Regulations, provide disciplines in this area. Trade facilitation is meant to increase transparency and to bring down these costs by streamlining and simplifying procedures and requirements and by providing technical assistance to improve infrastructure and train personnel. The Doha Declarations stipulate that there should first be a period of clarification and identification of needs and priorities of members, particularly developing countries. Only then a decision – by 'explicit' consensus – should be taken on whether to start negotiations. The DWP orders the Trade Negotiating Committee to establish a Negotiating Group on Trade Facilitation. The other nine paragraphs of the agreement on this issue cover technical assistance and support for capacity building. Moreover, it is made explicit that developing country members will not be obliged 'to undertake investments in infrastructure projects beyond their means'. If support for infrastructure projects is not forthcoming, implementation will not be demanded.[8]

The DWP is rather open on trade facilitation. Given the sensitivity of the Singapore Issues, this is understandable. The negotiations could develop an approach of tackling this trade barrier and take a first bite into it. Proposals made by members in 2004/05 are related to consultation with trading partners before introducing new regulations, appeal procedures, 'advance rulings', and technical assistance.

Other issues

With respect to intellectual property rights, much attention has been attracted by the separate declaration that was issued in Doha, according to which the TRIPS Agreement does not and should not prevent members from taking measures to protect public health.[9] The TRIPS Agreement should be interpreted in a manner supportive of public health, by promoting access to existing medicines, and research and development into new medicines. In August 2003, a decision of the General Council complemented this declaration in favour of developing countries that do not have pharmaceutical manufacturing capacity, permitting them to import generic versions of drugs still under patent protection at low prices. Moreover, the Doha Declarations spell out that negotiations will be held on a multilateral system of notification and registration of geographical indication for wines and spirits. In the DWP, the Director General is requested to continue his consultations on whether to expand the protection of geographical indications to other products. In 2001, the TRIPS Council was instructed to examine the relationship between the TRIPS Agreement and the Convention on Biological Diversity, the protection of traditional knowledge and folklore, and other issues raised by members. The development aspect was to be taken into account in these areas. However, the DWP does not explicitly mention these issues. Negotiations concentrate on patent protection of medicines and the use of genetic resources under disclosure of their origin or with 'prior informed consent'.

The Doha mandates of 2001 are confirmed by the DWP for rules on anti-dumping and countervailing measures in the case of subsidies. The WTO Ministers agreed to negotiations 'aimed at clarifying and improving disciplines' that have been formulated in the Uruguay Round Agreements on Article VI, Anti-dumping and Countervailing Duties. Fisheries subsidies are explicitly mentioned.

The clarification and negotiations on improvement of disciplines and procedures of GATT Article XXIV, Territorial Application – Frontier Traffic – Customs Unions and Free Trade Areas, and of the articles pertaining to dispute settlement will also continue under the DDA. The latter negotiations will have to find solutions for problems related to the follow-up of rulings by the Dispute Settlement Body (DSB): how to establish whether a ruling has been fully implemented, how to decide on sanctions, etc.

Environmental issues have been linked with trade negotiations for a long time. The Marrakesh Agreement brought the discussion into the WTO in a more formal way. The Doha Declarations go a step further by launching negotiations on some specific subjects and instructing the Committee on Trade and Environment to give particular attention to some issues. The DWP confirms that progress should be made in these issues.

After the conclusion of the DWP in early August 2004, negotiations are picking up steam. Concrete issues are now being addressed, such as the formulas for reduction of tariffs in trade in agricultural and manufactured products. There is now a real possibility that export subsidies in agriculture and comparable subsidies will be phased out. Technical assistance is coming forth to help developing countries to participate in the negotiations, and trade facilitation has been made conditional on the supply of aid. The deleting of three Singapore Issues from the agenda has made the negotiations more manageable. However, despite the progress that has been made, there are still some serious problems to be resolved before a 'single undertaking' can be put together that is sufficiently attractive for all WTO members.

The most important problem is finding a balance between a general formula for tariff reduction and exceptions for particular products. These exceptions could take the form of products kept outside the formula or to differentiated coefficients in the formula for developing countries. The issue of binding also plays a role here. Both developing and developed countries have made proposals for Sensitive and Special Products to be kept outside the workings of the formula. There is a real risk that the exceptions or differentiations agreed upon to reach a consensus will undermine and distort the type of trade liberalization that will result from the round. As far as SDT is the motive, longer implementation periods and technical assistance are to be preferred over exceptions. Sectoral protectionism in developed countries should be resisted outright.

The second major problem is keeping the countries on board that do not benefit from trade liberalization in the short or medium term. Net food-importing countries that do not have compensatory benefits (e.g. in the form of increased remittances of temporary migrants) are a case in point. The argument that these countries will benefit as a result of indirect effects will not be convincing for domestic constituencies. Benefits should be clear, particularly in the case of countries where a price increase of staple foods may even bring hunger to large segments of the population. Development aid might be included into the package in order to help particular countries to benefit more from the opportunities offered by a liberalized world economy.

A third major problem is the erosion of preferences. By supplying preferential systems within all kinds of frameworks, strong interests against non-discriminatory liberalization have been created. Cases in point are the Everything but Arms (EBA) initiative and the African Growth and Opportunity Act (AGOA). Erosion of preferential positions seems inevitable. By allocating preferences to the poorest countries only and by improving preferences by simplifying the systems and making the rules of origin less of a barrier, meaningful preferences may be offered in the years to come.

Many smaller obstacles stand in the way of a package deal that is acceptable as a 'single undertaking'. Given the substantial benefits that most countries will reap from a successful Doha Round, in the shape of increased welfare, jobs and growth, or in terms of a rules-based world trading order, it is not unrealistic to expect that the WTO members will in the end make a significant next step in the liberalization of world trade.

Notes

1 Deardorff and Stern (2003) counted the words 'development' and 'developing' 63 times in the 10 pages and 52 paragraphs of the Doha Declarations.
2 The Uruguay Round abolished the Multi-Fibre Arrangement that had managed trade in textiles and clothing by quantitative restrictions. However, high tariffs for

these products remain. The AoA was more important in that it introduced an approach for liberalization rather than for liberalization itself.

3 Egypt, Guinea, Morocco, and Mauritania are cases in point (WTO 2003: 136).

4 The general reduction will be complemented by product-specific caps on support.

5 The quantitative thresholds in this sentence are between brackets: 'binding level less than [35] per cent and expected to bind [100] per cent of their non-agricultural tariff lines.'

6 The limits of SDT have to be negotiated, as the brackets in the text show. Lower tariff cuts for up to [10] per cent of tariff lines and keeping up to [5] per cent of tariff lines unbound as long as they do not exceed [5] per cent of the imports of the member concerned.

7 The World Trade Report 2004 quotes a World Bank study indicating that in 2001, these remittances constituted 42 per cent of FDI inflows into developing countries (WTO 2004: 47).

8 However, the commitment for assistance is not 'open-ended'.

9 WTO, Ministerial Conference, Fourth Session, Doha, 9–14 November 2001, *Declaration on the TRIPS Agreement and Public Health.*

References

Acharya, R. and Daly, M. (2004) 'Selected issues concerning the multilateral trading system', Discussion Paper No. 7, Geneva: WTO.

Babarinde, O. and Faber, G. (2004) 'From Lomé to Cotonou: business as usual?', *European Foreign Affairs Review*, 9: 27–47.

Bridges Weekly Trade News Digest (2005), 9, No. 4.

Das, D.K. (2004) 'Free-trade rhetoric and reality', in *CESifo Forum*, 5: 3–9.

Deardorff, A.V. and Stern, R.M. (2003) 'Enhancing the benefits for developing countries in the Doha Development Agenda negotiations', Discussion Paper No. 498, Ann Arbor, MI: Gerald R. Ford School of Public Policy, University of Michigan.

Dijck, P. van (2000) 'Meeting Asia and Latin America in a new setting', in P. van Dijck and G. Faber (eds) *The External Economic Dimension of the European Union*, The Hague, London, and Boston, MA: Kluwer Law International.

Dijck, P. van (2002a) 'The EU's new strategies towards emerging Asia and Latin America', in K.W. Radtke and M. Wiesebron (eds) *Competing for Integration. Japan, Europe, Latin America, and their Strategic Partners*, Armonk, NY: M.E. Sharpe.

Dijck, P. van (2002b) 'Economic achievements and challenges ahead', in P. van Dijck and M. Wiesebron (eds) *Ten Years of Mercosur, Cuadernos del Cedla No. 9*, Amsterdam.

Dijck, P. van and Faber, G. (eds) (2000) *The External Economic Dimension of the European Union*, The Hague, London, and Boston, MA: Kluwer Law International.

Faber, G. (2002) 'Deepening of multilateral integration in the World Trade Organization', in K.W. Radtke and M. Wiesebron (eds) *Competing for Integration. Japan, Europe, Latin America, and their Strategic Partners*, Armonk, NY: M.E. Sharpe.

Finger, J.M. and Schuler, P. (2000) 'Implementation of Uruguay Round commitments: the development challenge', *The World Economy*, 23: 511–526.

Francois, J., Meijl, H. van, and Tongeren, F. van (2002) 'Economic benefits of the Doha round for the Netherlands', report submitted to the Ministry of Economic Affairs, The Hague.

GATT (1994) *The Results of the Uruguay Round of Multilateral Trade Negotiations. The Legal Texts*, Geneva: GATT Secretariat.

Hoekman, B., Ng, F., and Olarreaga, M. (2002) 'Eliminating excessive tariffs on exports of least developed countries' *The World Bank Economic Review*, 16: 1–21.

Hoekman, B., Ng, F., and Olarreaga, M. (2004) 'Agricultural tariffs or subsidies: which are more important for developing countries?' *The World Bank Economic Review*, 18: 175–204.

Primo Braga, C.A., Fink, C., and Paz Sepulveda, C. (2002) 'Intellectual property rights and economic development', *World Bank Policy Research Working Paper No. 412*, Washington, DC: The World Bank.

Rood, J. (2000) 'Transatlantic economic relations in a new era', in P. van Dijck and G. Faber (eds) *The External Economic Dimension of the European Union*, The Hague, London, and Boston, MA: Kluwer Law International.

Srinivasan, T.N. (2002) 'Developing countries and the multilateral trading system after Doha', *Center Discussion Paper No. 842*, New Haven, CT: Yale University, Economic Growth Center.

WTO (2001a) 'Ministerial Declaration', Ministerial Conference, Fourth Session, Doha, 9–14 November.

WTO (2001b) 'Declaration on the TRIPS Agreement and Public Health', Ministerial Conference, Fourth Session, Doha, 9–14 November.

WTO (2003) *World Trade Report 2003*, Geneva: World Trade Organization.

WTO (2004) *World Trade Report 2004*, Geneva: World Trade Organization.

WTO (n.d.) *Market Access: Unfinished Business*, Special Study No. 6, Geneva: WTO.

2 Global trade reform and the Doha Development Agenda

Kym Anderson, Will Martin and Dominique van der Mensbrugghe

Introduction

While the negotiations on the Doha Development Agenda (DDA) have been proceeding for over three years, there remains considerable uncertainty about what will be achieved. While there is interest in the substantial potential gains from reform, there is concern in many quarters about the potential adverse impact on protected sectors, and about potential collateral impact on net-food-importing countries and those countries heavily reliant on trade preferences. While some important progress was made in July–August 2004 with the adoption of a Doha Work Programme (DWP), there is much uncertainty about how it will be implemented (WTO 2004).

Despite this uncertainty, the DWP does provide some key features of the final modalities that allow purposeful investigation of tradeoffs and possibilities. In particular, it proposes that liberalization of both tariffs and domestic support be undertaken from current bound levels using tiered formula approaches with larger cuts on higher rates of protection. It also specifies that members should be able to designate some tariffs as 'sensitive'. The purpose of this chapter is to examine the potential impact of liberalization, and to explore some of the trade-offs within the range of liberalization possibilities laid out in the DWP. We draw heavily on the detailed assessment presented in Anderson *et al.* (2005).

While model-based assessments of the impact of global trade liberalization have been available for some time, most of these models have not been able to take account of important real-world phenomena such as tariff preferences. Many databases have also ignored the non-*ad valorem* tariffs that provide the bulk of industrial-country protection to agriculture. The recent release of Version 6 of the Global Trade Analysis Project (GTAP) database rectifies this problem by incorporating tariff information that includes all major preference arrangements. See www.gtap.org for more details. Like earlier versions of the GTAP database, it also incorporates the protective impacts of the specific elements of tariffs – an issue that is particularly important given the heavy reliance of the industrial countries on non-transparent specific tariffs for agricultural protection.

In this chapter, we shall first examine the potential impact of comprehensive trade reform, the abolition of all trade-distorting trade measures including import tariffs, export subsidies, and domestic support. Next, we shall examine the key elements of the DWP agreement, and the possible implications of different degrees of liberalization consistent with that framework.

Potential impact of global trade liberalization

We undertake this analysis using the LINKAGE model of the global economy maintained at The World Bank (Van der Mensbrugghe 2004a). This model builds on the GTAP database and has much in common with the GTAP model although it has some key distinguishing characteristics. See Hertel (1997) and www.gtap.org. A key difference is that it is recursive dynamic, so while it starts with 2001 as its base year it can be solved annually through to 2015. The dynamics are driven by exogenous population and labour supply growth, savings-driven capital accumulation, and labour-augmenting technological progress. In any given year, factor stocks are fixed. Producers minimize costs subject to constant returns to scale production technology, consumers maximize utility, and all markets – including for labour – are cleared with flexible prices. There are three types of production structures. Crop sectors reflect the substitution possibility between extensive and intensive farming. Livestock sectors reflect the substitution possibility between ranch versus range feeding. All other sectors reflect standard capital-labour substitution with two types of labour: skilled and unskilled. There is a single representative household per modelled region, allocating income to consumption using the extended linear expenditures system. Trade is modelled using a nested Armington structure in which aggregate import demand is the outcome of allocating domestic absorption between domestic goods and aggregate imports, and then aggregate import demand is allocated across source countries to determine the bilateral trade flows.

The most important form of protection in the model is import tariffs, represented by a set of bilateral tariffs on agricultural and non-agricultural products. There are also bilateral export subsidies. Domestically, there are subsidies only in agriculture, where they apply to intermediate goods, outputs, and payments to capital and land.

Three closure rules are used. First, government fiscal balances are fixed in any given year.[1] The fiscal objective is met by changing the level of lump-sum taxes on households. This implies that losses of tariff revenues are replaced by higher direct taxes on households. Second, the current-account balance is fixed. Given that other external financial flows are fixed, this implies that *ex ante* changes in the trade balance are reflected in *ex post* changes in the real exchange rate. For example, if import tariffs are reduced, the propensity to import increases. Additional imports are financed by increasing export revenues and this is typically achieved by a real exchange rate depreciation. Finally, investment is savings driven. With fixed public and foreign savings, investment will be driven by two factors: changes in the savings behaviour of households and changes in the unit costs of investment. The latter can play an important role in a dynamic model if imported capital goods are taxed. Because the capital account is exogenous, rates of return across countries can differ over time and across simulations. The model only solves for relative prices. The *numéraire*, or price anchor, in the model is given by the export price index of manufactured exports from high-income countries. This price is fixed at unity in the base year and throughout time.

The latest version of the LINKAGE model, Version 6.0, is based on the latest release of the GTAP dataset, Release 6.05.[2] Compared with Version 5 of the GTAP dataset, Version 6 has a 2001 base year instead of 1997, updated national and trade data and, importantly, a new source for the protection data. The new protection data on tariff bindings and applied rates come from the MAcMap joint project between Centre d'Etudes Prespectives et d'informations Internationales (CEPII), Paris and International Trade Centre (ITC), Geneva (Bouët *et al.* 2004), and a CEPII project on tariff bindings (Bchir *et al.* 2005). This provides a detailed database on bilateral protection that integrates applied and bound rates; trade preferences, specific tariffs and a partial evaluation of non-tariff barriers (NTBs), for example tariff rate quotas (TRQs).[3] In summary, the new GTAP database has lower tariffs than the previous database because of the inclusion of bilateral trade preferences and of major reforms between 1997 and 2001 such as continued implementation of the Uruguay Round Agreement and China's progress towards WTO accession, which contributed to the global exports plus imports-to-GDP ratio rising from 44 to 46 per cent over those four years (see Van der Mensbrugghe 2004b).

The version of the LINKAGE model used for this study is a 27-region, 25-sector aggregation of the GTAP data set. See Appendix Table A12.2 in Anderson *et al.* (2005). There is a heavy emphasis on agriculture and food, comprising 13 of the 25 sectors, and a focus on the largest commodity exporters and importers. See Annex 2.1 for definitions of regions.

The main source of protection is tariffs, although some countries – particularly high-income countries – also have significant agricultural production and export subsidies. The average import tariff for agriculture and food is 16.0 per cent for developed countries and 17.7 per cent for developing countries, while for manufactures other than textiles and clothing it is 8.3 per cent for developing countries and just 1.3 per cent for developed countries, although there is a great deal of variation around these averages. See Anderson *et al.* (2005), Appendix Table A12.8.

The impact of complete, global trade reform on each of the regions is shown in Table 2.1, together with the impact of terms of trade changes on the net benefits to the region. For regions where the main source of gains is liberalization by other countries, the terms-of-trade gains are likely to be large relative to the overall gains. For regions where world prices of imports rise, however, terms-of-trade effects are likely to be negative. Table 2.1 shows that the total estimated gains from that reform would generate 287 billion US dollars in additional income in 2015, with two-thirds of those global gains accruing to high-income countries. However, as a share of income, developing countries, as self-defined by WTO members, do somewhat better, with an average increase of 1.2 per cent, compared to 0.6 per cent for developed countries.

Table 2.1 Impact on real income from full liberalization of global merchandise trade, by country and region, 2015

	Impact in 2015 relative to the baseline in billions of 2001 US dollar		As % of baseline income
	Real income effect	Terms of trade effect	
Australia and New Zealand	6.1	3.5	1.0
EU 25 plus EFTA	65.2	0.5	0.6
USA	16.2	10.7	0.1
Canada	3.8	−0.3	0.4
Japan	54.6	7.5	1.1
Korea and Taiwan	44.6	0.4	3.5
Hong Kong and Singapore	11.2	7.9	2.6
Argentina	4.9	1.2	1.2
Bangladesh	0.1	−1.1	0.2
Brazil	9.9	4.6	1.5
China	5.6	−8.3	0.2
India	3.4	−9.4	0.4
Indonesia	1.9	0.2	0.7
Thailand	7.7	0.7	3.8
Vietnam	3.0	−0.2	5.2
Russia	2.7	−2.7	0.6
Mexico	3.6	−3.6	0.4
South Africa	1.3	0.0	0.9

Table 2.1 Continued

	Impact in 2015 relative to the baseline in billions of 2001 US dollar		As % of baseline income
	Real income effect	*Terms of trade effect*	
Turkey	3.3	0.2	1.3
Rest of South Asia	1.0	−0.8	0.5
Rest of East Asia	5.3	−0.9	1.9
Rest of LAC	10.3	0.0	1.2
Rest of ECA	1.0	−1.6	0.3
Middle East and North Africa	14.0	−6.4	1.2
Selected SSA countries	1.0	0.5	1.5
Rest of Sub-Saharan Africa	2.5	−2.3	1.1
Rest of the world	3.4	0.1	1.5
Developed countries	201.6	30.3	0.6
Developing countries (WTO definition)	141.5	−21.4	1.2
Developing countries	85.7	−29.7	0.8
Middle-income countries	69.5	−16.7	0.8
Low-income countries	16.2	−12.9	0.8
East Asia and Pacific	23.5	−8.5	0.7
South Asia	4.5	−11.2	0.4
Europe and Central Asia	7.0	−4.0	0.7
Middle East and North Africa	14.0	−6.4	1.2
Sub-Saharan Africa	4.8	−1.8	1.1
Latin America and Caribbean	28.7	2.2	1.0
World total	287.3	0.6	0.7

Source: Authors' The World Bank LINKAGE model simulations.

Note
For country groupings see Annex 2.1.

From Table 2.1, it is clear that the potential benefits from global liberalization of merchandise trade are large and widely distributed. However, the benefits clearly vary widely across developing countries, ranging from little impact in the case of Bangladesh and Mexico to 4 or 5 per cent increases in parts of East Asia. The second column shows the amount of that welfare gain due to changes in the international terms of trade for each country. For developing countries as a group the terms-of-trade effect is negative, reducing somewhat the gains from improved efficiency of domestic resource use, especially in China and India. Of particular interest are the implications for the three groups of countries from Sub-Saharan Africa. Each of these groups – South Africa, Selected Sub-Saharan African countries, and the Rest of Sub-Saharan Africa – makes worthwhile gains, both in absolute terms and as a share of baseline income. This is despite the widely held concerns about the effects of preference erosion and rising costs of imported goods that are incorporated in the model, and reflects the improvements in market access, and reductions in the costs of own trade barriers associated with global trade reform.

There are several ways to decompose the real income gains from global trade reform so as to better understand the sources of these gains. One key issue is the impact of liberalization by different groups of countries; another is the impact by policy instrument. The latter decomposition, focusing on the controversial pillars of the agriculture agreement, gave results very similar to those reported in Hertel and Keeney (2005), namely that market access barriers explain almost all the welfare effects of agricultural policy reform, with domestic support and export subsidy removal playing only a very minor role and in fact slightly harming developing countries as a group, since some food-importing developing countries gain from farm export subsidies in high-income countries. In our case all but about 1 per cent of the global welfare gains from full removal of all merchandise trade barriers and agricultural subsidies is due to import tariff cuts, which is also what Hoekman *et al.* (2004) estimated from halving all agricultural distortions while making a partial equilibrium analysis. Hertel and Keeney's estimate from full liberalization of all merchandise markets was only slightly higher, at 4.6 per cent (see their Table 2.7). While the negotiators have rightly placed considerable emphasis on reducing the highly distorting export subsidies and domestic support in the high-income countries, it clearly should be borne in mind that the real income gains to developing countries come very predominantly from reductions in market access barriers.

As to the decomposition by sector, our results are provided in Table 2.2. They suggest global liberalization of agriculture and food yields 62 per cent of the total global gains, similar to Hertel and Keeney's 66 per cent. This is consistent with the high tariffs in agriculture and food (16.7 per cent global average) versus other sectors, but is nonetheless remarkable given the low shares of agriculture in global Gross Domestic Product (GDP) (4 per cent)

Table 2.2 Regional and sectoral sources of gains from full liberalization of global merchandise trade, developing and developed countries, 2015

	Change in real income in 2015 relative to baseline scenario					
	In billions of 2001 US dollar			*As % of global gain*		
	Developing	*Developed*	*World*	*Developing*	*Developed*	*World*
Developing countries liberalize:						
Agriculture and food	30	19	49	10	6	16
Textiles and clothing	9	12	21	3	5	8
Other merchandise	6	52	58	2	19	21
All sectors	45	83	128	15	30	45
Developed countries liberalize:						
Agriculture and food	26	107	133	9	37	46
Textiles and clothing	15	2	17	5	1	6
Other merchandise	4	5	9	1	2	3
All sectors	45	114	159	15	40	55
All countries liberalize:						
Agriculture and food	56	126	182	19	43	62
Textiles and clothing	24	14	38	8	6	14
Other merchandise	10	57	67	3	21	24
All sectors	90	197	287	30	70	100

Source: Authors' The World Bank LINKAGE model simulations.

Note
Small interaction effects are distributed proportionately and numbers are rounded to sum to 100 per cent.

and global merchandise trade (9 per cent). Three-quarters of the gains from agricultural liberalization are accounted for by the farm policies of high-income countries. Notice too that in the case of developing countries, even more of their gain from farm reform is due to South–South agricultural liberalization (30 billion US dollars) than to increased access to markets of developed countries (26 billion US dollars). That is almost equally true in the case of the manufacturing sector in aggregate, despite the big gains

Table 2.3 Impact of full global merchandise trade liberalization on real factor prices, percentage change in 2015 relative to the baseline in 2001

	Unskilled wages	*Skilled wages*	*Capital user costs*	*Land user costs*	*CPI**
Australia and New Zealand	3.1	1.1	−0.3	17.4	1.2
EU 25 plus EFTA	0.0	1.3	0.7	−45.4	−1.3
USA	0.1	0.3	0.0	−11.0	−0.4
Canada	0.7	0.7	0.4	22.8	−0.9
Japan	1.3	2.2	1.1	−67.4	−0.1
Korea and Taiwan	6.5	7.1	3.8	−45.0	−0.7
Hong Kong and Singapore	3.2	1.6	0.3	4.4	1.1
Argentina	2.9	0.5	−0.7	21.3	0.3
Bangladesh	1.8	1.7	−0.2	1.8	−7.2
Brazil	2.7	1.4	1.6	32.4	2.2
China	2.2	2.2	2.8	−0.9	−0.4
India	2.8	4.6	1.8	−2.6	−6.0
Indonesia	3.3	1.5	0.9	1.0	0.5
Thailand	13.2	6.7	4.2	11.4	−0.6
Vietnam	25.3	17.6	11.0	6.8	−2.3
Russia	2.0	2.8	3.5	−2.2	−3.3
Mexico	2.0	1.6	0.5	2.8	−1.4
South Africa	2.8	2.5	1.8	5.7	−1.6
Turkey	1.3	3.4	1.1	−8.1	−0.3
Rest of South Asia	3.7	3.2	0.1	0.1	−2.7
Rest of East Asia	5.8	4.2	5.2	−0.9	−1.6
Rest of LAC	5.7	1.4	−0.4	17.8	−1.2
Rest of ECA	2.3	4.2	2.1	−0.3	−2.6
Middle East and North Africa	4.1	4.1	2.6	2.4	−3.1
Selected SSA countries	6.0	1.6	0.0	4.6	0.4
Rest of SSA	8.2	6.5	2.2	5.2	−5.0
Rest of the world	4.4	2.7	1.1	6.3	−1.4
Developed countries	0.6	1.1	0.5	−20.0	−0.6
Developing countries	3.5	3.0	1.9	0.9	−1.7
Middle-income countries	3.2	2.6	1.9	2.2	−1.1
Low-income countries	4.2	3.9	1.9	−1.0	−4.0
World total	1.2	1.5	0.8	−0.8	−0.8

Note
* CPI = Consumer Price Index.

from textiles and clothing reform: 15 billion US dollars from market access in high-income countries compared with 9 billion US dollars due to growth of South–South trade in textiles. Put differently, reform by developing countries is nearly as important in terms of economic welfare gains to the South as reform by developed countries.

The relatively small percentage changes in net national economic welfare hide the fact that redistributions of welfare among groups within each country following trade reform can be much larger. This is clear from the impact on real rewards to labour, capital and land that are reported in Table 2.3. The results also strongly support the expectation from trade theory that returns to land and unskilled labour would rise substantially in developing countries, and by more than wages of skilled workers, which in turn rise more than returns to capital. This reform therefore would improve equity and reduce poverty in those countries, given that the vast majority of the poor are farmers or unskilled labourers in those countries. For developed countries, again consistent with standard trade theory, skilled workers gain more than unskilled workers. Owners of land and other capital are estimated to gain least.

Impact of partial reforms

The DDA, like all other multilateral negotiations, cannot be expected to achieve full free trade. The DWP sets out some relatively specific approaches to liberalization in the most vexed area of agriculture, and less specific objectives in the case of non-agricultural market access. In what follows, we examine the likely implications of partial liberalization broadly within the framework set out by the DWP. We consider in particular the possible interpretation of a tiered formula, and the specification for the Sensitive and Special Products to be subjected to special treatment. Finally, we consider the implications of alternative degrees of Special and Differential Treatment (SDT) in market access liberalization.

Specifying tiered formulas

The DWP is consistent with economic theory in seeking to reduce the highest – and economically most costly – tariffs by the most. It does this using a tiered formula whose details are unspecified. If this were interpreted as a tariff reduction formula that applied higher proportional cuts to higher tariff rates, it would introduce a potentially serious problem. Such a formula involves major discontinuities at the points where higher proportional cuts begin. Figure 2.1 illustrates the nature of the problem for a tiered formula where tariffs of 15 per cent or less are subject to cuts of 40 per cent; tariffs between 15 and 90 per cent are subject to cuts of 50 per cent; and tariffs over 90 per cent are subject to cuts of 60 per cent. Such discontinuities are

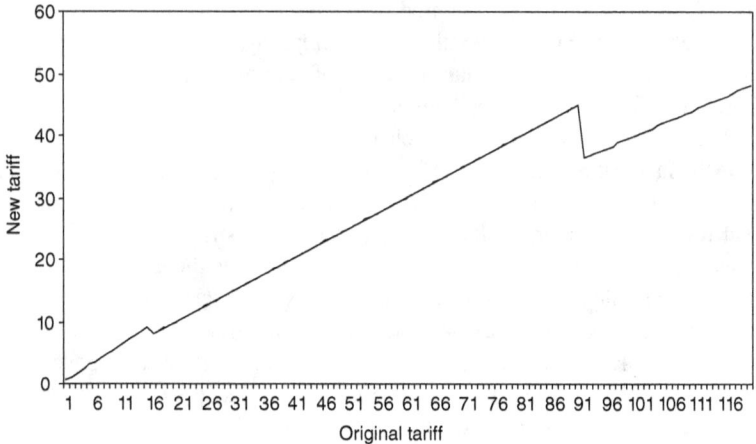

Figure 2.1 Converting the Harbinson formula into a tiered formula.

not just an analytical inconvenience – they can be expected to create major resistance to reform from industries just above the discontinuity.

One coherent solution to this problem canvassed by Jean *et al.* (2005) is to follow the approach of progressive tax systems, in which the higher rates of cut apply only to the component of the target variable that exceeds the threshold level. The resulting mapping from initial tariff rates to final tariff rates is depicted in Figure 2.2. This avoids discontinuities, at the expense of making somewhat smaller cuts in the higher tariffs, because the part of these tariffs below the threshold values are cut at lower rates.

Specifying Sensitive Products

A second key issue in the context of agricultural tariff cuts is the provisions in the DWP allowing members to self-designate a certain number of Sensitive Products, and developing country members to designate, in addition, a number of Special Products. The number of these products is to be negotiated, so information on the impact of designating different numbers of such products should be relevant to decisions on the number of such products permitted. While market access in Sensitive Products is to be expanded through a combination of tariff cuts and expansion of TRQs, the intent of this designation is clearly to allow the retention of higher levels of protection than would be the case through application of the tiered formula. Moreover, there is clear evidence in De Gorter and Kliauga (2005) that liberalization through expansion of TRQs has widely been thwarted by quota administration methods.

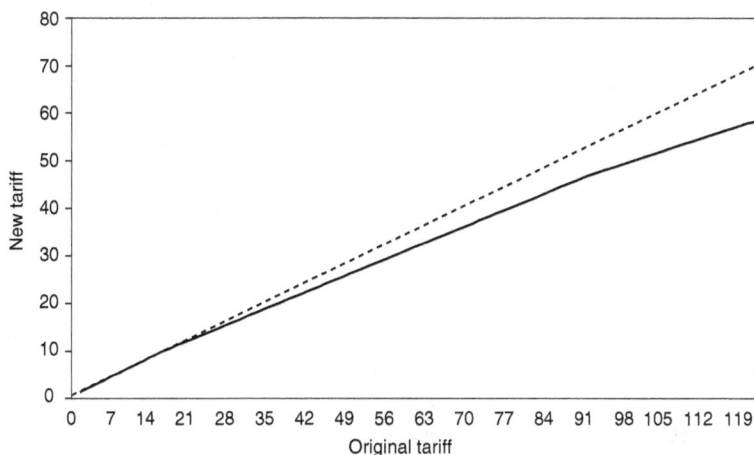

Figure 2.2 A tiered tariff-cutting formula without discontinuities.

It seems reasonable to assume that, in choosing which products to specify as sensitive, policy makers will take into account the extent to which the tiered formula being applied would cause politically painful cuts in applied tariffs. They also seem likely to take into account the importance of the goods being imported. While they could use their limited number of allowed Sensitive Products to protect some small products with high tariffs, it seems more likely that they would use them to shelter tariffs on goods that are important in production and trade, rather than tariffs on products of minor importance.

In light of these considerations, Jean *et al.* (2005), selected the products to be treated as sensitive by taking into account the extent to which their applied tariff rates would be reduced – taking into account both the height of the applied rate and the extent to which that tariff was sheltered from cuts by a substantial gap between the applied rate and the tariff binding. They also took into account the importance of the product, as proxied by the initial volume of imports. This effectively meant choosing the products that would otherwise have suffered the largest reduction in tariff revenues.

Special and Differential Treatment

While there are many dimensions of SDT in the WTO as discussed by Hoekman *et al.* in Chapter 6 of this volume, there are two key dimensions in the negotiations on market access in agriculture and non-agriculture.

The first issue is the depth of the cuts to be undertaken by developing countries, and the second is the specification of Special Products.

In the Uruguay Round, developing countries were to make smaller reductions in their tariffs than the developed countries. In agriculture, this was formalized as a goal of a 36 per cent average cut in agricultural tariffs in industrial countries, and a 24 per cent cut in developing countries.[4] In manufactured products, the approach was less formulaic, since the negotiations used a combination of request-and-offer and zero-for-zero negotiations. However, Abreu (1996) estimated the reduction in average applied tariffs to be 38 per cent in developed countries and 25 per cent in developing countries – suggesting that tariffs for manufactured products in developing countries were cut by roughly two-thirds as much as cuts in developed countries. Given the importance of precedent in international trade negotiations, it seems reasonable to specify developing country tariff cuts as two-thirds as large as those in developed countries.

The specification of Special Products is more complex, since the preconditions for these products – food security, livelihood security, and rural development – are not well defined (WTO 2004). If Sen's (1981) view that food security is determined by whether people are able to obtain the food they need is accepted, protection may well reduce food security. While livelihood security raises more complex issues, the balance of evidence from current research on trade and poverty (Hertel and Winters 2005) suggests that trade liberalization generally reduces poverty, and that the key to poverty reduction lies much more in policies focused directly on the earnings of the poor. In practice, the effect of allowing additional exceptions for Special Products seems likely to reduce the extent of liberalization in a manner similar to the Sensitive Products demanded by some developed countries.

Some potential Doha partial liberalization scenarios

In this study, we first consider a pre-scenario designed to move the tariff base from the 2001 tariffs appearing in Version 6 of the GTAP model to the tariffs that would have applied in the absence of a WTO round. This involves reducing tariffs in line with those Uruguay Round commitments extending beyond 2001, the accession commitments to phase in tariff reductions, especially in China (Bhattasali *et al.* 2004), and the recent expansion of the European Union (EU) to 25 countries.

Following this pre-experiment, we report six partial liberalization scenarios – detailed in Table 2.4 – the first four of which focus on agricultural liberalization. The first is the application of a tiered formula of the type discussed in the previous section. The second introduces Sensitive Products. The third examines the implications of a Proportional Cut approach to tariff cutting that reduces higher tariffs by more in absolute, but not relative, terms – an

Table 2.4 Specification of the Doha liberalization scenarios

Pre-simulation	Amends 2001 protection measures by allowing EU eastward enlargement to 25 members, implementation of WTO accession commitments by China, and implementation of Uruguay Round commitments including abolition of quotas on textiles and clothing by the end-of 2004, followed by normal global growth projection for ten more years to 2015 (baseline simulation).
Scenarios	All scenarios assume agricultural domestic support cuts in developed countries and the abolition of agricultural export subsidies, plus:
Tiered	Tiered formula for agricultural market access with cuts in bound tariffs of 45% below 15%, 70% between 15 and 90%, and 75% above 90%; for developing countries the marginal cuts were 35, 40, 50, and 60% and the transition points 20, 60, and 120%; no cuts for LDCs. Cuts in newly acceding countries 2/3 of cuts in other developing countries.
Sensitive	Tiered + Sensitive Products (2% for developed countries and 4% for developing countries). Tariff bindings for sensitive products cut by 15%.
Proportional	Proportional cut in agricultural tariffs of developed countries (with 33% cuts for developing countries and none for LDCs) to get the same cut in the average tariff as in Tiered.
Sensitive + Cap	Tiered + 2% sensitive products + reductions in high tariffs down to a 200% tariff cap.

Note
For country groupings see Annex 2.1.

approach that might conceivably make it easier to reach agreement. The fourth scenario combines a tiered formula with Sensitive and Special Products with a tariff cap of 200 per cent. The fifth scenario adds a 50 per cent cut in non-agricultural tariffs to the original tiered-formula approach to agricultural market access. The final scenario assumes a 50 per cent proportional cut in non-agricultural tariffs for developing and developed countries.

Impact on agricultural tariffs

A key factor in understanding the impact of each of these scenarios on the world economy, and particularly on developing countries, is their effects on agricultural tariffs. In the industrial countries, these tariffs are much higher than those on industrial products, much more variable across products, and much less transparent, and – as noted earlier – have been found to be the most influential in terms of potential welfare impacts.

In Table 2.5, we show in the first column that the average tariff on agricultural and food products[5] would be 15.2 per cent in the absence of

Table 2.5 Doha scenarios: average applied tariffs for agricultural products, by country and region, in percentages

	Baseline		Tiered	Sensitive	Proportional	Sensitive + Cap	Tiered + NAMA	Doha-All
	2001	Pre-simulation						
Australia and New Zealand	2.6	2.6	1.7	2.3	1.3	2.3	1.7	1.7
EU 25 plus EFTA	13.9	13.9	7.2	11.2	7.0	11.1	7.0	7.0
USA	2.4	2.4	1.7	2.2	1.4	2.2	1.7	1.7
Canada	9.0	9.0	4.9	8.1	5.2	8.1	4.9	4.9
Japan	29.4	29.3	15.2	25.5	16.7	21.7	14.7	14.7
Korea and Taiwan	55.0	53.0	28.4	45.3	32.4	29.8	27.9	18.7
Hong Kong and Singapore	0.1	0.1	0.1	0.1	0.1	0.1	0.1	0.1
Argentina	7.1	7.1	6.9	7.1	6.7	7.1	6.9	6.1
Bangladesh	12.7	12.7	12.7	12.7	12.7	12.7	12.7	11.9
Brazil	5.0	5.0	4.9	5.0	4.9	5.0	4.9	4.4
China	37.6	10.3	8.2	9.1	7.9	9.1	7.9	6.9
India	50.3	49.9	45.5	47.9	45.0	47.9	45.5	37.4
Indonesia	5.0	5.0	4.9	5.0	4.8	5.0	4.9	4.5
Thailand	29.7	16.7	13.9	15.1	13.2	15.1	13.5	11.0

Vietnam	37.1	37.1	37.1	37.1	37.1	37.1	37.1	37.1
Russia	13.5	13.5	8.8	10.9	7.8	10.9	8.7	6.5
Mexico	11.6	10.3	8.6	10.0	8.3	10.0	8.6	6.5
South Africa	8.8	8.6	8.1	8.5	7.9	8.5	8.1	6.6
Turkey	16.7	16.6	13.8	15.8	13.8	15.8	13.8	10.6
Rest of South Asia	21.3	21.1	20.9	21.1	20.7	21.1	20.9	16.5
Rest of East Asia	13.7	13.4	12.7	13.2	12.8	10.3	12.7	11.2
Rest of LAC	11.0	10.8	9.8	10.3	9.5	10.3	9.8	8.9
Rest of ECA	16.0	15.7	14.3	14.9	14.0	14.9	14.3	12.9
Middle East and North Africa	14.1	13.1	11.6	12.6	11.6	12.6	11.5	10.4
Selected SSA countries	11.9	11.8	11.6	11.8	11.6	11.8	11.5	11.0
Rest of SSA	21.4	21.2	19.6	20.8	19.7	20.8	19.6	16.1
Rest of the world	12.1	11.8	11.5	11.7	11.6	11.5	11.5	9.4
Developed countries	16.0	15.9	8.4	13.5	8.9	11.5	8.2	7.5
Developing countries	17.7	14.2	12.5	13.4	12.3	13.3	12.4	10.6
Dev. countries (WTO)	20.0	16.9	13.1	15.5	13.3	13.9	13.0	10.7
Middle-income countries	16.5	12.1	10.4	11.4	10.1	11.2	10.3	8.9
Low-income countries	22.2	22.0	20.7	21.5	20.7	21.5	20.7	17.5
World total	16.7	15.2	10.0	13.5	10.3	12.2	9.9	8.8

a Doha agreement. The cut in applied agricultural tariffs resulting from the tiered formula used in this chapter is surprisingly modest given that the formula used is much more ambitious than seems generally to be envisaged. The average applied rate would be cut by 5.2 percentage point, from 15.2 to 10.0 per cent. Among the main economies or groups shown in Table 2.5, only the EU 25 plus European Free Trade Area (EFTA), Japan, Korea, and Taiwan (China) display more than a 5 percentage point cut in applied duties. For many countries applied duties are hardly changed. Roughly half the economies shown in Table 2.5 experience a decline in applied duties of less than 1 percentage point. For Pakistan, for instance, there is a 47 percentage points cut in the average bound duty, but this translates into a 0.5 point cut in the average applied duty. Sub-Saharan African countries have to make only relatively small cuts in their tariffs, and least-developed countries (LDCs) make no cuts at all. Given the extent of the binding overhang in developing countries, the formula considered only narrows the binding overhang in many cases, without substantially changing applied duties.

The effects of allowing 2 per cent of tariff lines to be treated as sensitive are quite spectacular. The average reduction in tariffs falls from 5.2 to a mere 1.7 percentage points – a third of the original cut, and this with only 2 per cent Sensitive Products. The reductions in the tariff cut are very large in the EU, Japan, Korea, Taiwan (China), and EFTA. Only in Korea and Taiwan (China) is there any significant reduction in tariffs after the inclusion of Sensitive Products. While developing countries suffer a little less political 'pain' from their own tariff cuts, they face large reductions in their 'gain' from improved market access when the industrial countries no longer need to reduce their tariffs. In the case of China, for instance, the reduction in the tariffs facing China falls from 14.8 to 3.4 percentage points, while the reduction in China's own tariffs falls from 2.1 to 1.2 percentage points.

The sharp reduction in the required cut in industrial countries' average tariffs follows from the fact that the Sensitive Products are restricted by a number of tariff lines, rather than by the value of trade or another more relevant criterion. When Jean *et al.* (2005) investigated further, they found that the reduction in average tariff cuts is much less serious when Sensitive Products are constrained as a percentage of trade, than as a percentage of tariff lines. Ideally a better approach to constraining the flexibility involved with Sensitive Products could be identified (Tyers 2005), but moving from the number of tariffs to the value of trade appears to help balance flexibility and discipline.

The Proportional Cut scenario is designed to bring about the same reduction in average tariffs in developed and developing countries as the tiered formula. This scenario reduces the higher tariffs by less than the tiered formula, and lower tariffs by more. Thus, the reduction in Japan's tariffs falls from 14.1 percentage points to 12.6, while that for the Southern African Customs Union (SACU) rises from 0.5 to 0.7 percentage points. The coefficient of variation of each country's tariffs also declines by less than under the tiered formula. While it is desirable from an economic viewpoint to lower high tariffs more than low tariffs, the difference between the Proportional Cut scenario and the Tiered Formula scenario seems relatively small. The Proportional Cut approach meets the general requirement in the DWP of reducing higher tariffs by more – in absolute terms – than lower tariffs. This suggests that a Proportional Cut approach might be useful in future negotiations, should it prove difficult to reach agreement on larger proportional cuts in higher tariffs.

The next scenario includes the tiered formula with 2 per cent Sensitive Products, and a tariff cap of 200 per cent. This scenario reduces the losses in terms of market access associated with allowing Sensitive Products: the reduction in average agricultural tariffs declines from 5.2 to 3 percentage points, rather than to 1.7 percentage point in the absence of the cap. The cuts under this scenario fall more heavily on Japan than under any other scenario, because of the extremely high protection provided to a few commodities in Japan.

The final scenario in Table 2.5 shows the effects of treating all developing countries in the same way as developed countries. While we recognize that this approach has next to no chance of success, it seems worthwhile to examine the consequences of this full-participation scenario. This reduces the global average tariff by 6.4 percentage points, rather than 5.2 percentage points under the regular tiered formula, and hence increases market access overall. The tariff reductions in many developing countries increase substantially in percentage points, with India's average tariff rate, for instance, declining by 12.5 percentage points as against 4.4 percentage points under the standard tiered formula. Non-LDCs in Africa also experience larger reductions in tariffs, with the cut rising from 2.8 percentage points to 7.6 percentage points. While such large cuts would clearly generate some political pain, it is important to examine their impacts in terms of economic gain.

Welfare impact of partial liberalization

The welfare impacts of the liberalization scenarios are shown in Table 2.6. These scenarios focus on the agricultural tariff cuts discussed earlier, but also include the abolition of the export subsidies contained in the GTAP model, and reductions in domestic support according to a tiered formula under which countries with domestic support above 20 per cent of the value of production face cuts of 75 per cent (Jensen and Zobbe 2005).

Table 2.6 Doha scenarios: change in real income in 2015, in billions of 2001 US dollars, relative to the baseline in 2001

	Tiered	Sensitive	Proportional	Sensitive + Cap	Tiered + NAMA	Doha-All
Australia and New Zealand	2.0	1.1	2.2	1.2	2.4	2.8
EU 25 plus EFTA	29.5	10.7	28.2	10.9	31.4	35.7
USA	3.0	2.3	3.4	2.1	4.9	6.6
Canada	1.4	0.5	1.2	0.4	0.9	1.0
Japan	18.9	1.8	15.1	12.9	23.7	25.4
Korea and Taiwan	10.9	1.7	7.3	15.9	15.0	22.6
Hong Kong and Singapore	−0.1	−0.1	−0.1	−0.2	1.5	2.2
Argentina	1.3	1.0	1.4	1.0	1.3	1.6
Bangladesh	0.0	0.0	0.0	0.0	−0.1	−0.1
Brazil	3.3	1.1	3.2	1.1	3.6	3.9
China	−0.5	−1.5	−0.4	−1.1	1.7	1.6
India	0.2	0.2	0.1	0.2	2.2	3.5
Indonesia	0.1	0.2	0.2	0.0	1.0	1.2
Thailand	0.9	0.6	1.0	0.8	2.0	2.7
Vietnam	−0.1	0.0	−0.1	−0.1	−0.5	−0.6
Russia	−0.3	−0.7	−0.1	−0.7	0.8	1.5
Mexico	−0.2	−0.3	−0.2	−0.3	−0.9	−0.2
South Africa	0.1	0.3	0.1	0.3	0.4	0.7
Turkey	0.6	0.0	0.5	0.0	0.7	1.4
Rest of South Asia	0.2	0.1	0.2	0.2	0.3	0.7
Rest of East Asia	0.1	0.0	0.1	1.0	0.3	0.6
Rest of LAC	3.7	0.5	3.7	0.4	3.9	4.0
Rest of ECA	−0.2	−0.3	−0.2	−0.2	−0.6	−0.7
Middle East and North Africa	−0.8	−1.2	−0.9	−1.2	−0.6	0.1
Developed countries	65.6	18.1	57.2	43.2	79.9	96.4
Developing countries (WTO definition)	19.7	1.2	16.3	16.8	32.6	47.7
Developing countries	9.0	−0.4	9.1	1.1	16.1	22.9
Middle-income countries	8.0	−0.5	8.3	1.0	12.5	17.1
Low-income countries	1.0	0.1	0.8	0.0	3.6	5.9
East Asia and Pacific	0.5	−0.8	0.9	0.6	4.5	5.5
South Asia	0.4	0.3	0.3	0.4	2.5	4.2
Europe and Central Asia	0.1	−0.9	0.2	−0.9	0.8	2.1
Middle East and North Africa	−0.8	−1.2	−0.9	−1.2	−0.6	0.1
SSA	0.3	0.0	0.3	−0.1	0.4	1.2
LAC	8.1	2.3	8.0	2.1	7.9	9.2
World total	74.5	17.7	66.3	44.3	96.1	119.3

Source: Authors' The World Bank LINKAGE model simulations.

They reveal that application of the tiered formula, without exceptions, would yield global benefits of 74.5 billion US dollars per year, roughly a quarter of the benefits from global trade reform reported in Table 2.1. Of this gain, approximately 9 billion US dollars would accrue to low- and middle-income countries – just one-tenth of the potential gains from complete global liberalization. Part of this difference arises from the smaller reductions in developing country tariffs relative to those in developed countries. As can be seen from Table 2.5, agricultural tariffs in developing countries fall by just over 10 per cent of their initial level under the tiered formula, while they fall by almost half in developed countries. The smaller reductions in developing countries' tariffs mean that they experience a much smaller share of the benefits from reform.

Moving from full liberalization as depicted in Table 2.1, to partial agricultural liberalization with smaller cuts in developing country bound rates (and *a fortiori* in developing country applied rates) in Table 2.6, strongly reduces the gains to developing countries. The overall gains to low and middle-income countries as a group fall from 85.7 billion US dollars in Table 2.1 to 9 billion US dollars in Table 2.6. The gains to each developing country region fall sharply, with those to countries in Africa declining from 4.8 billion US dollars to roughly 0.3 billion US dollars, and the Middle East and North Africa experiencing a small loss. Only Latin America and the Caribbean experiences sizeable gains. The focus of the WTO on liberalization that goes beyond agriculture is clearly important for securing sufficient gains to developing countries.

Moving to the Sensitive scenario, the gains to developing countries become negative. This largely appears to be a consequence of smaller reductions in industrial countries' tariffs. Instead of declining by 7.5 percentage points, agricultural tariffs in high-income countries drop by only 2.4 percentage points, substantially reducing the market access gains to low- and middle-income countries. Developing countries' own agricultural tariffs also fall by less, with the cut shrinking from 1.7 to 0.8 percentage point, and this reduces their gains from improving the efficiency of their own agricultural trade regimes.

In the Proportional Cut scenario, without Sensitive Products, developing country gains overall return to levels comparable with those under the Tiered Formula scenario. When the tiered formula and Sensitive Products are combined with a cap of 200 per cent, the global welfare gains rise from 17.7 billion US dollars under the Sensitive scenario to 44.3 billion US dollars, but the gains to developing countries remain extremely small.

When Non-Agricultural Market Access (NAMA) liberalization is included in the analysis, the global gains rise from 74.5 billion to 96.1 billion US dollars, and the gains to developing countries rise from 9.0 billion to 16.1 billion US dollars. There are worthwhile gains to most developing countries under this scenario, and the exceptions appear to have relatively clear explanations, such as preference erosion in the cases of Bangladesh and Mexico.

The final scenario, Doha-All, involves developing countries liberalizing using the same tiered formula as the industrial countries in agriculture, and the same proportional cuts to non-agricultural tariff bindings. This scenario generates aggregate gains of 119.3 billion US dollars, or 42 per cent of the potential gains from abolition of all the trade barriers under consideration. The gains to developing countries are 22.9 billion US dollars, still only a quarter of the estimated potential gains from full trade reform. This reflects largely the much smaller reductions in applied tariffs in developing countries than in the industrial countries – a consequence of the much larger tariff-binding overhang in developing countries relative to the developed countries.

Conclusions

Liberalization of global merchandise trade has the potential to increase world real incomes by around 287 billion US dollars using conventional, static measures of changes in real income. Of this total gain, just over 60 per cent arises from removal of agricultural market access barriers, with the remainder arising primarily from removal of tariffs on textiles and clothing (14 per cent) and with other merchandise tariffs providing the rest of the gain. Removal of agricultural domestic support and export subsidies generates only around 1 per cent of the total welfare gains, despite their considerable symbolic importance. These measures are much smaller than market access barriers, and some export subsidies, in particular, generate benefits to some developing countries. Of the total benefits from complete global liberalization, around one-third would accrue to developing countries, even after allowance is made in this study for the effects of preferences, and the impact of rising food prices on some poor food-importing countries. The gains from global trade reform to developing countries would be twice as large relative to initial incomes as those accruing to the industrial countries.

In this chapter, we analysed a series of partial reform scenarios based on the DWP. These scenarios involve partial liberalization of tariffs, domestic support in agriculture, and agricultural export subsidies. The liberalization of tariffs and domestic support are undertaken using tiered formulas that impose larger cuts on relatively higher levels of support.

An aggressive tiered formula in agriculture, with a top marginal rate of tariff cutting of 75 per cent yields a reduction in global tariffs on agricultural and food products of 5.2 percentage points. With smaller tariff cuts in developing countries, and much wider gaps between bound and applied rates, the reductions in applied tariffs are smaller. This scenario generates welfare gains of 74 billion US dollars, around a quarter of the gains from full global liberalization. Of this, only about 9 billion US dollars in gains accrues to developing countries, in large part because the reductions in their own tariffs are smaller, and hence they reap smaller efficiency gains, and smaller gains in access to markets of other developing countries.

Allowing even 2 per cent of Sensitive Products to be subjected to much smaller cuts than the tiered formula (we use 15 per cent cuts in bound rates) would cause the market access gains from the tiered formula to virtually disappear. In this case, the reduction in average agricultural tariffs would fall to 1.7 percentage points, and the global welfare gains to 17.7 billion US dollars, with a small loss to developing countries. These results clearly imply a need for Sensitive-Product treatment to be used with extreme care – either by constraining the products to be classified as sensitive, or by ensuring substantial improvements in market access for these goods.

Alternative approaches to liberalization are considered in the chapter, including proportional cuts in agricultural tariffs, and use of a cap of 200 per cent on tariffs. The proportional approach yields slightly smaller cuts in higher tariffs, and slightly smaller welfare gains than a tops-down formula. A tariff cap reduces the losses resulting from the Sensitive Product provisions.

Adding access reforms for non-agricultural products substantially increases the global gains, and the gains to developing countries: adding NAMA increases the global gains from reform by 28 per cent, to 96.1 billion US dollars, but raises the gains to developing countries by 78 per cent. Inclusion of NAMA also increases the number of developing countries that benefit overall from the outcome of the negotiations.

Another change that would greatly increase the gains to developing countries is fuller participation in the reforms. If developing countries undertook the same cuts in bound tariffs as the industrial countries, their gains would rise from 16 billion to 22.9 billion US dollars. This scenario yields global welfare gains of 119 billion US dollars, or 41 per cent of the potential gains from complete trade reform. In contrast with the complete abolition of trade barriers, the gains to developing countries remain much smaller, because binding overhang in developing countries reduces the extent of the reductions that they bring about in their applied rates – the rates that are most relevant for determining the economic costs of a trade regime. However, the combination of wider reforms by inclusion of NAMA and deeper cuts in developing countries' tariffs generates substantially larger and more widely distributed gains to developing countries than the scenarios involving only agricultural reforms, and with liberalization diminished by use of exceptions for Sensitive and Special Products.

Annex 2.1 Country groupings in the GTAP 6

Rest of Europe and Central America (ECA): Albania, Bulgaria, Croatia, Romania, and Rest of former Soviet Union.

Latin America and the Caribbean (LAC): Argentina, Brazil, Mexico, and Rest of LAC.

Rest of LAC: Chile, Colombia, Peru, Uruguay, Venezuela, Rest of Andean Pact, Rest of South America, Central America, Rest of FTAA, Rest of the Caribbean.

Rest of South Asia: Sri Lanka and Rest of South Asia.

Rest of East Asia: Malaysia and the Philippines.

Selected Sub-Saharan Africa (SSA): Botswana, Malawi, Mozambique, Tanzania, Zambia, Zimbabwe, Madagascar, and Uganda.

Rest of SSA: Rest of South African Customs Union, Rest of SADCC, and Rest of Sub-Saharan Africa.

For more information see the GTAP website, www.gtap.org

Notes

1 For the sake of simplicity they are fixed in US dollar terms at their base year level, minimizing potential sustainability problems. This implies they decrease as a percentage of GDP for expanding economies.

2 The Global Trade Analysis Project (GTAP) is an international consortium of trade researchers at universities, research institutions, and national and international agencies. The GTAP Centre, based at Purdue University, provides four key resources to the trade community. First and foremost is an integrated and consistent international database for trade policy analysis. The current version is composed of 87 country/region groupings and 57 economic sectors. The second is a publicly available global trade model, also known as the GTAP model. Note that the LINKAGE model is distinct from the GTAP model though it uses the same underlying database. The third is an annual course in applied trade modelling. And finally, GTAP organizes and co-hosts the annual Conference on Global Economic Analysis. More information on the GTAP Centre and project can be found at http://www.gtap.agecon. purdue.edu

3 More information on the MAcMap database is available in Bouët *et al.* (2004) and at http://www.cepii.fr/anglaisgraph/bdd/macmap.htm

4 Lamentably, the average cut is a meaningless metric. A 99 per cent cut in a 1 per cent tariff plus a 99 per cent cut in a 100 per cent tariff yields a 50 per cent average cut, but essentially no improvement in market access.

5 Agricultural and food products are here defined at the level of products used in the GTAP modelling. This results in slightly different estimates from those presented by Jean *et al.* (2005), who aggregate from the six-digit level of the Harmonized System to agricultural products as defined by the WTO.

References

Abreu, M. (1996) 'Trade in manufactures: the outcome of the Uruguay Round and developing country interests', in W. Martin and L.A. Winters (eds) *The Uruguay Round and the Developing Countries*, Cambridge: Cambridge University Press.

Anderson, K., Martin, W. and Van der Mensbrugghe, D. (2005) 'Market and welfare implications of Doha reform scenarios', in K. Anderson and W. Martin (eds) *Agricultural Trade Reform and the Doha Development Agenda*, manuscript, Washington, DC: The World Bank.

Bchir, M., Jean, S. and Laborde, D. (2005) 'Binding overhang and tariff-cutting formulas: a systematic, worldwide quantitative assessment', CEPII no. working paper 2005–2013, Paris: CEPII.

Bhattasali, D., Li, S. and Martin, W. (eds) (2004) *China and the WTO Accession, Policy Reform and Poverty Reduction*, Washington, DC: Oxford University Press and The World Bank.

Bouët, A., Decreux, Y., Fontagné, L., Jean, S. and Laborde, D. (2004) 'A consistent, *ad valorem* equivalent measure of applied protection across the world: the MAcMap-HS6 database', 20 December, mimeo, Paris: CEPII.

Gorter, H. de and Kliauga, E. (2005) 'Reducing tariffs versus expanding tariff rate quotas', in W. Martin and K. Anderson (eds) *Agricultural Trade Reform and the Doha Development Agenda*, manuscript, Washington, DC: The World Bank.

Hertel, T. (ed.) (1997) *Global Trade Analysis: Modeling and Applications*, New York: Cambridge University Press.

Hertel, T. and Keeney, R. (2005) 'What's at stake: the relative importance of import barriers, export subsidies and domestic support', in W. Martin and K. Anderson (eds) *Agricultural Trade Reform and the Doha Development Agenda*, manuscript, Washington, DC: The World Bank.

Hertel, T. and Winters, L.A. (2005) *Putting Development Back Into the Doha Agenda: Poverty Impacts of a WTO Agreement*, manuscript, Washington, DC: The World Bank.

Hoekman, B., Ng, F., and Olarreaga, M. (2004) 'Agricultural tariffs or subsidies: which are more important for developing countries?' *The World Bank Economic Review*, Vol. 18, No. 2, pp. 175–204.

Jean, S., Laborde, D. and Martin, W. (2005) 'Consequences of alternative formulas for agricultural tariff cuts' in W. Martin and K. Anderson (eds) *Agricultural Trade Reform and the Doha Development Agenda*, manuscript, Washington, DC: The World Bank.

Jensen, H. and Zobbe, H. (2005) 'Consequences of reducing domestic support limits', in W. Martin and K. Anderson (eds) *Agricultural Trade Reform and the Doha Development Agenda*, manuscript, Washington, DC: The World Bank.

Martin, W. (2004) 'Market access in agriculture: beyond the blender', Trade Note No. 17, Washington, DC: The World Bank. Available online at www.worldbank.org (accessed on 14 October 2005).

Mensbrugghe, D. van der (2004a) 'LINKAGE technical reference document: version 6.0', mimeo, Washington, DC: The World Bank.

58   *Kym Anderson* et al.

Mensbrugghe, D. van der (2004b) 'Comparison of GTAP release 5.4 and GTAP release 6.05', mimeo, Washington, DC: The World Bank.

Sen, A. (1981) *Poverty and Famines: An Essay on Entitlement and Deprivation*, Oxford: Clarendon Press.

Tyers, R. (2005) 'Implicit policy preferences and trade reform by tariff aggregates', mimeo, Washington, DC: The World Bank.

WTO (2004) 'Doha work programme: decision adopted by the general council on 1 August 2004', WT/L/579, Geneva: World Trade Organization (The July Framework Agreement).

3 Modelling global trade reform

Some reflections

Michiel Keyzer

The model

Chapter 2 of this volume by Anderson, Martin, and Van der Mensbrugghe provides only a brief description of the model that has been used to analyse the impact of several scenarios to liberalize trade in the context of the Doha Development Agenda (DDA). As pointed out, the model is recursively dynamic, with savings financing capital stock accumulation, and makes ample use of the Armington assumption under a CES technology so as to reflect product heterogeneity across countries. As this is not the occasion to give detailed comments on the model, only some brief remarks are made.

First, on a positive note, it seems far better to use a general equilibrium model as is the case here than to follow the practice of the Organisation for Economic Cooperation and Development (OECD) of making Producer Support Estimates (PSEs). Notwithstanding all its limitations, a general equilibrium model actually shows the impact of reform, while the PSEs do not even attempt to measure the welfare gains that could be obtained from a reform.

Second, with all due qualifications, the outcomes presented seem plausible as outcomes of this type of model. Indeed, world models are bound to suffer from serious limitations, since the representation of any region or country in the world necessarily is grossly simplified. Moreover, it is not clear that refining some of the regional models while keeping the others in their present state, would improve the overall outcomes, and it would definitely not help transparency.

Finally, with respect to the status of this dynamic model, I would think that simulation outcomes should only be circulated once the model has been calibrated over its historical period, in particular with respect to price developments on the world market and growth in output of the various commodities, by region. It seems that so far the model was only calibrated statistically for a single year, 2001, for a version with 27 sectors and

25 regions. Substantial differences in outcomes between several versions of the model raise serious concerns about the numerical robustness of the model outcomes: in the 2005 version, presented in Chapter 2 of this volume, full liberalization yields welfare gains of 287 billion US dollars, which is 123 billion US dollars less than was the case in the version of June 2004.

Scenario simulations

The thrust of the study by Anderson *et al.* is to assess the implications of six scenarios, the first four of which focus on agricultural trade liberalization alone, comparing

i   a tiered formula for agricultural market access to implement the concept stated in the Harbinson document for reducing bound tariffs;
ii   allowing for exemptions for Sensitive Products;
iii   proportional cuts in agricultural tariffs;
iv   proportional cut combined with a tariff cap of 200 per cent;
v   tiered formula plus 50 per cent cut in bindings on non-agricultural tariffs and
vi   a tiered formula for developed countries in agriculture and a 50 per cent proportional cut in bindings on Non-Agricultural Market Access (NAMA) for all countries.

Turning to the scenario specification, the presentation is rather explicit about the various forms of tariff cuts that could be envisaged but far less about how these are actually implemented in the simulations presented. Indeed, the discussion of the simulations suggests that most of the findings largely follow directly from the arithmetic of the tariff formulae used in a particular scenario and far less from the response of the model. It is, for example, clear that the Tiered-reduction scenario (i) is governed by the fact that the bound tariffs to be lowered under the agreement are often so much higher than the applied tariffs actually affecting domestic market prices, that the impact of cutting bound tariffs is only noticeable in few markets. There is no need for a model to establish such a fact. On the contrary, it would have been informative to present tables showing the gap between bound and applied tariffs and the partial effect of reducing the bound level before turning to simulations. Similarly, there is hardly a need for an equilibrium model to establish in scenario (ii) that allowing for a certain percentage of tariff lines to be exempted from the tariff cuts on the ground of being a Sensitive Product yields even less liberalization, and that this protectionist effect is mitigated if the exemption is on a certain percentage of import value. Here too it is hard to envisage how the commodity detail of the real world regulation can be represented in the 27-sector model with Armington import functions. The presentation does not offer much clarification in this respect. Furthermore, despite the numerous references to real-world policies, the text remains unclear about the way tariffs on processed foods are dealt with.

With respect to the numerical findings for which the model is essential, reference is made to Table 2.2 of the Anderson *et al.* chapter, an excerpt from which is shown in Table 3.1.

The following conclusions may be drawn from these scenario studies.

Gains mostly accrue to the bloc that liberalizes

To start with, Table 3.1 shows, not unexpectedly, that the deeper the reform the higher the gain. Even clearer is the fact that the gains mostly accrue to the bloc that liberalizes. Developed countries gain most from their liberalization, and more if they also liberalize deeper. Other countries also gain more when they participate in the reform.

Indeed, in the logic of the model used, which is characterized by rather imperfect substitution between home and foreign goods (Armington assumptions), the main loser from protection is the home economy, the consumer in particular. Since the model does not represent the difficulties in raising taxes, it would be much easier in developed countries to help farmers through direct income transfers than by way of border protection. As farmers constitute an almost negligible fraction of the population it is quite inefficient to let all home consumers face distorted prices for their sake. The lesson has been taught quite often: in money terms developed country consumers are the main victims of protectionism.

Table 3.1 Real income gains from agricultural and non-agricultural trade reform, in billions of 2001-US dollars, 2015

| | Change from baseline | | | |
| | *All countries liberalize* | | *Developed countries liberalize* | |
	Non-agricultural trade reform	*Agricultural trade reform*	*Non-agricultural trade reform*	*Agricultural trade reform*
Developed countries	71	126	7	107
Developing countries	34	56	19	26
World total	105	182	26	133

Source: Computed from this volume, Chapter 2, Table 2.2.

Developing countries gain most from liberalization of South–South trade and not from liberalization of north only

The second point, which is consistent with the first observation, is that developing countries hardly gain from reform in the developed countries only and mainly profit when they liberalize themselves. That is the logic of this model, which clearly shows in the figures, not only in developed countries but also in the developing world. The implication for the Doha package is that all good things start at home, including trade reform. This presumably is to a great extent due to the model structure but it typically is a conclusion that developing country negotiators may not like.

Maximum gain less than 4 per cent of income rise over 2000–15

Third, the table shows that the largest attainable welfare gain as measured in terms of real income is only 287 billion US dollars. Note that this is not an annual increment but the total gain achieved in 2015 of a recursively dynamic model with capital accumulation. Now contrast this with the total world income in 2002 of about 30,600 billion US dollars that, in a conservative estimate, will grow at 1.5 per cent annually. Then, the total gain from full liberalization amounts to less than one year of growth and less than 4 per cent of the total rise in income over that period, which exceeds 7,600 billion US dollars. Taking into account the vagaries of economic cycles, this almost implies that even the largest gain is insignificant. What are we talking about if this is all we can get from our efforts? Hence, it would seem that the mere statement that the gains are 'purely static' may not be sufficient to fence off the criticism, especially since the model is said to be dynamic. In particular, the following qualifications might be of relevance.

No measurement of the gains for the poor

When it comes to poverty alleviation, the macro numbers presented cannot tell us much, precisely because the very poor almost vanish in the sea of revenues earned by the rich, and hence in their welfare differentials across simulation runs. The authors might try to make this more visible, even though it is accepted that the methodology used does not allow identifying the poor within countries or country blocs. Yet, one could expect that some of the gains, in particular those related to reduction of tariffs on processing, might be pro-poor. However, as mentioned earlier the simulations do not refer to these aspects.

A static model despite some dynamic features

A maximum welfare gain as measured in real income of 287 billion US dollars resulting from liberalization after 15 years of a run with a dynamic model is not very promising. The bleak achievement is presumably due to the fact that the model is essentially static, because it does not include the technical progress and structural change induced by market reforms. China offers a prime example of how market orientation with adequate government infrastructural investments can trigger growth once human capital is available. Such growth is not agriculture-led, nor is it heavily dependent on relative prices between agriculture and the rest of the economy and even less on prices within agriculture. In the rural sector, the growth of meat production and food processing in the 1990s was effective because of the rising purchasing power in the cities. This made it possible to achieve some growth in rural areas and, by keeping the reserve labour force in rural areas satisfied, also to maintain sufficient political stability to allow for industrialization in the urban areas without an explosion of migration to the main centres. In short, the focus of trade models on relative prices distracts from the triggers of market reform and the human and infrastructural resource base that really matters in the medium term.

Again, this is not a criticism of the structure of the model itself, as this type of world model cannot accommodate most of such factors except through 'fudge factors' that do create dynamic gains but at the same time enables one to fully manipulate the model outcomes. The authors deserve to be commended for not resorting to easy tricks to boost up the gains. Indeed, very often the critical triggers are only known with hindsight.

Nonetheless, one could expect of a model that carries the seal of approval of reputed international organizations that it be calibrated on a reasonably long period in the past, rather than on the single year 2001, so as to at least reproduce the savings and accumulation path. Moreover, the dynamic aspects of market reform might be put into better perspective in the text, which currently seems too pessimistic.

Prospects for a development package

Good prospects for meat, dairy, and feed grains

China offers the best opportunity for growth. Through its increased demand for animal proteins, China offers great opportunities for exports of either meat and dairy or feed grain from whomever can supply these. In fact, developed countries, Europe and Japan in particular, with their satiated demand and aging population would seem to offer far less interesting markets for potential exporters in the future. In contrast to this, the reforms in Central and Eastern Europe will trigger additional supply and make it interesting for Europe to expand its dairy, meat, and feed grain exports to Asia, currently mainly China. The authors might point this out more explicitly, highlighting the interests of developed countries as agricultural exporters in the future. Moreover, towards the end of the simulation period of this study, India might follow suit and offer additional outlets. Here is a potential for South–South trade that might be emphasized.

Bleak prospects for unprocessed tropical products

Unfortunately, the regions that can benefit from this are few. Outside the temperate zones of Latin America, countries in the South have limited prospects to participate, as China and India have ample opportunity to produce tropical products including palm oil, sugar, and cotton by themselves. Partly because of the incomplete dynamic calibration, the modelling part of the study may be too optimistic on the long-term trends in raw material prices for tropical products. Between 1970 and 2000, prices of sugar, cotton, coffee, and cocoa decreased by 30 to 60 per cent in nominal terms, that is not even accounting for inflation. For these products, this would seem to confirm the Prebisch hypothesis that technical progress in production and demand satiation causes world market prices of primary commodities to decline persistently. For these products, volatility and downward trends in prices do not stem from protection of farmers in developed countries – sugar and cotton are protected strongly – but are rather the result of low price elasticity and demand satiation. Developing countries compete fiercely as suppliers and the increase in production by one often goes at the expense of the others and depresses prices as well, leaving developed country consumers as main beneficiaries. Cynics have said that in this respect as well, the WTO only helps the developed world. Indeed, there is a serious danger that for tropical products, trade liberalization would only accelerate this downward trend in prices. This holds for instance with respect to sugar and cotton, where an open market would make it attractive for China to expand its present investments in its Southern regions that face serious unemployment, and out-compete all others on the world market.

In short, as far as raw materials are concerned, export prospects seem favourable for those countries that can produce animal feed, but they are bleak for other countries. The implication for the Doha package is that unlike in Cancun, it might be wise for individual developing countries to maintain alliances only with countries that share their interests. Tropical countries stand little to gain from lowering import tariffs on dairy products and cereals in developed countries. They should focus on what they have in common: the capacity to produce tropical products.

Gains from dismantling of tariff escalation in agricultural processing

On an average, industrial countries' tariffs on agricultural products reach 4.6 per cent for raw materials, 8.3 per cent for semi-processed products, and 11 per cent for fully processed agricultural commodities, and not only for products that include agricultural raw materials that are protected within the European Union (EU). For example, the EU has no import tariff on unprocessed cocoa, but a 21 per cent bound tariff rate on processed cocoa, and even for countries belonging to the African, Caribbean and Pacific (ACP) group of countries with special and preferential trade relations with the EU, applied tariffs are around 20 per cent (EU applied tariff database: http://mkaccdb.eu.int/cgi/-bin/wtdar.pl).

This is remarkable as these rates are much higher than rates for industrial products are, and this holds even for processed goods that do not contain any agricultural product that could compete with temperate-zone goods. The phenomenon can only be explained as a vestige from colonial times, which has survived in the shade of agricultural protection. Enabling tropical countries to participate more actively in the processing chain is the only way for them to speed up their rural development. Therefore, relocation of parts of processing chains to developing countries seems needed. Lower tariffs of course give no assurance that the processing industry will actually find it profitable to relocate to developing countries, but judging by their present resistance to tariff reduction, it would seem that developed countries have something to fear in this respect.

There should be no illusion that for goods with significant value added in processing – that is: for goods where escalation matters – the gains would ever accrue in full to the farmers through higher sales volumes and better prices. Irrespective of competition worldwide, the processing sector would definitely get hold of the bulk of the rent, essentially because farmers by their very location in rural areas never have direct access to world markets. For high value-added products they will continue being paid in accordance with their revenue on the next-best product at the farm prices that can meet this given demand. In modelling terms, this also amounts to an equilibrium representation but one that pays attention to the institutional properties of price transmission through processing chains. The model is not equipped to represent this and it would be very difficult to overcome this limitation in this study.

Figure 3.1 gives an illustration of the phenomenon. Besides cocaine, there hardly is a market where intervention has been stronger in recent years than tobacco (Keyzer and Weesenbeeck 2004). Yet, despite all anti-smoking campaigns, the tobacco-producing farmers worldwide have not seen much change in their prices. On a positive note, for products with high value processing and satiated demand, price volatility on world markets is not an issue for farmers.

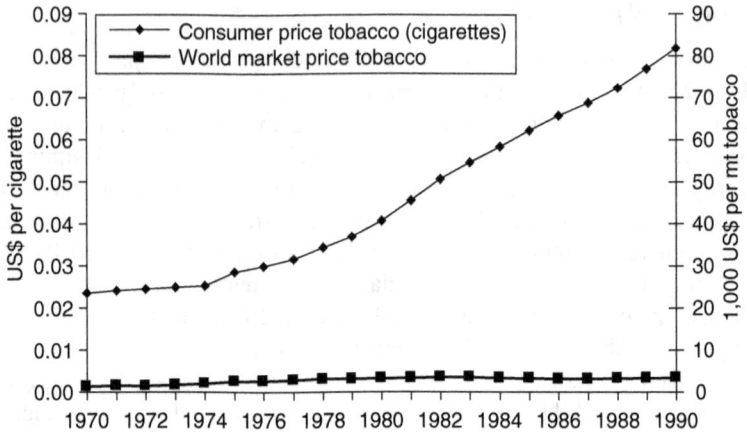

Figure 3.1 Price transmission in the tobacco chain, 1970–90.

Sources: FAO (2003) Projections of tobacco production, consumption and trade to the year 2010, Rome: FAO; Stewart, M.J. (1993) 'The effect of advertising bans on tobacco consumption in OECD countries', *International Journal of Advertising*, 12: 155–180.

The figure shows that the intervention hardly influenced world market prices for tobacco. The low price elasticity of consumer demand implies that higher taxation on the consumption of tobacco products does not lead to significantly lower pre-tax prices, and the chain of transmission is therefore already broken at a very high retail level. The small decrease in profits for retail and wholesale can be easily cushioned through a slight fall in the margins without affecting the world market for raw tobacco. However, the final link from world market prices to farm prices is somewhat blurred by the fact that the EU and the USA have kept elaborate producer subsidy programs in place and that the anti-smoking campaigns have in one way or the other been going on for quite some time already. Additional information on farm prices for tobacco in some tobacco-producing developing countries suggests that the volatility in farm prices is more pronounced than that in world market prices, as shown in Figure 3.2.

Agricultural lobbies in developed countries have recently brought forward the argument of limited price transmission to the farmers in discussions on reform of the sugar sector under the motto 'Why help Brazilian elites to the detriment of Europe's farmers?' The argument is not valid because Brazilian cultivators may benefit even if the price increase on the world sugar markets resulting from trade liberalization does not permeate through to them. It admittedly remains hard to predict what will happen after

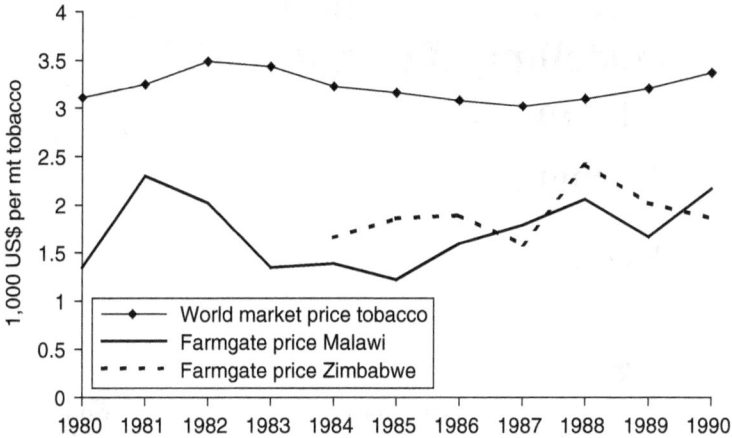

Figure 3.2 World market prices and farm gate prices for tobacco, selected countries, 1980–90.

Source: FAO (2003) 'Projections of tobacco production, consumption and trade to the year 2010', Rome: FAO.

liberalization but the experience with the tobacco and cocaine chains suggests that the processors would, as long as their margin remains large enough, effectively shield farmers from price fluctuations and other large shocks in the world market, and possibly also provide some insurance against climatic variability. In addition, processing can expand the market outlets for agriculture, offer additional employment for the rural population, and generate export revenues at prices that would hopefully remain on more favourable terms than for the raw materials themselves.

References

Keyzer, M.A. and Wesenbeeck, C.F.A. van (2004) 'Changed market access in the North and the farm prices in the South: some lessons from the war on drugs', *De Economist*, 152: 543–560.

4 Market access and the modelling of global trade reform

A comment

Joseph Francois

Introduction

The latest round of multilateral trade negotiations in the World Trade Organization (WTO) has been struggling with a poorly defined agenda. Some of the most important issues yet to be resolved are in tariff reduction modalities, including the modalities for agricultural liberalization. Chapter 2 of this volume by Anderson, Martin and Van der Mensbrugghe explores some of the issues related to market access, with an emphasis on agriculture. As such, it is a welcome addition to the information on the Doha Development Agenda (DDA).

Quantifying the economic impact of a WTO agreement is massively complex, even when it comes to issues as straightforward as tariff and subsidy cutting. The eventual agreement on the DDA should lower thousands of individual tariffs in each of the 150 or so WTO member countries. The result would be important shifts in resources among sectors in most countries, along with attendant changes in the prices of goods and factors of production. We should also expect shifts in countries that do not liberalize themselves, because of changes in world prices. With international trade, the supply and demand factors in each country will directly and indirectly affect resource allocation in all other countries. How can economists evaluate the impact of these choices? The most practical way of proceeding is to employ a large-scale computable general equilibrium model that allows simultaneous consideration of all the effects. This is the approach adopted in Chapter 2.

The focus here will be on three worrying aspects of the negotiation process as it is evolving, and how these critical issues are handled. This includes (i) the issue of trade preferences; (ii) the question to what extent we can really expect any tariff reductions at all by developing countries; (iii) the weight placed on agriculture in the overall context of the WTO negotiations.

Trade preferences

Non-reciprocal trade preferences have been long granted by developed countries to various developing countries. Early in the post-Second World War history of the system of the General Agreement on Tariffs and Trade (GATT), the pattern of these preferences reflected past colonial trade ties. In 1968, the UN Conference on Trade and Development (UNCTAD) recommended the creation of a Generalized System of Preferences (GSP) under which industrialized countries would grant trade preferences to all developing countries on a non-reciprocal basis. While UNCTAD has addressed a wider spectrum of issues in international economic relations, in the area of international trade its primary goal was to modify the most-favoured nation (MFN) clause underpinning the GATT by (partially) exempting developing countries from this obligation, while at the same time encouraging developed countries to discriminate in favour of imports from developing countries. A key principle was and still is the idea that such 'Special and Differential Treatment' be granted on the basis of 'non-reciprocity', reflecting the premise that 'treating unequals equally simply exacerbated inequalities' (UNCTAD 2004).

The jury remains out on whether trade preferences have actually made a substantive difference in terms of enhancing the welfare of recipient countries. Among the developing countries that were granted the fewest preferences at its inception in the 1960s, those in East Asia have subsequently grown the fastest. Conversely, those granted the deepest preferences, including least-developed countries (LDCs) in Sub-Saharan Africa, have not managed to increase their income per capita or diversify their export bundles significantly in the last 40 years. To a large extent both developments – rapid and sustained growth in Asia and the absence thereof in much of Africa – are not due to trade policies of developed countries, but rather reflect domestic policies and institutions. Most would agree that the major constraint on export diversification and expansion in Africa is on the supply side.

Whatever the intended and actual impact of trade preferences, they are a central issue in ongoing efforts to negotiate further multilateral trade liberalization. Middle-income countries are increasingly concerned about the discrimination they confront in markets of developed countries as a result of the better access granted in these markets to other industrialized countries – because of free-trade agreements – and to poorer or 'more preferred' developing countries. Conversely, preferences are used as an argument by the LDCs and African countries against a general liberalization of trade and removal of trade-distorting policies in agriculture – these countries worry about the potential negative effects of an erosion of their preferential access.

Chapter 2 is part of an emerging set of research based on recent data, which include the actual scope of preferences in trade. This is not a simple task, and one does not really appreciate the effort involved in building the data set on which the study rests. The import protection data used are based on a thorough and careful effort to include use of preferences in a matrix of global import protection (Bouet *et al.* 2004). These data are the product of a joint effort between the UN International Trade Centre, UNCTAD, the WTO and the Paris-based Centre d'Etudes Prospectives et d'Informations Internationales (CEPII). An important contribution of this project has been an exhaustive coverage of preferential trade agreements (PTAs) across the world, combined with calculation of the *ad valorem* equivalents of specific duties. Combined with differences in the bilateral composition of trade, the result is that protection varies by sector and partner for each importer. These data have in turn been integrated with the database of the Global Trade Analysis Project (GTAP) for 2001. The authors have imposed the elimination of quotas on textiles and clothing on the benchmark, an event which occurred on 1 January 2005, as laid down in the Uruguay Round Agreement on Textiles and Clothing. This is of course an important dimension of preference erosion in its own right, insofar as the constraint on the most efficient producers under the Agreement on Textiles and Clothing implied there was an implicit preference for the non- or less-constrained developing country exporters.

Given the preference dimension in Chapter 2, the authors have addressed a broad criticism of this literature. However, they do not tell us if it actually makes a difference or not. This is disappointing. Recent work suggests that while it matters for some countries for some sectors, overall there is not really much actual overall value to LDCs from preferences. Rather, the system tends to help some countries by hurting others, dividing developing countries as they fight over the rents involved and creating opposition to the general process of market integration and trade liberalization. This has been an important feature of the agricultural negotiations, and further discussion would have been welcome in this context.

Scope for actual liberalization

Chapter 2 notes that in the Uruguay Round, developing countries had a lesser set of obligations *vis-à-vis* tariff reductions. Reference is then made to Abreu (1996), who estimated that developing country reductions may have been deeper than developed country reductions. However, this is all based on tariff bindings. Bindings are the legal commitments entered in the GATT/WTO by members, and places an upped bound on tariff rates. The reality is that in agriculture bound rates are often far above applied rates for all WTO Members,

Table 4.1 Applied tariff rates for manufacturing after a 50 per cent reduction in bindings, Brazil, India, and Thailand, in percentages

	Current average applied tariff	Binding overhang	Reduction in average applied tariff
Brazil	15.9	14.9	15.4
India	19.2	3.9	41.3
Thailand	10.5	7.8	31.6

Source: Francois *et al.* (2005).

while in manufacturing this is the case for most developing countries. The result is that we all greatly overestimated the implications for applied rates in the Uruguay Round. In the current situation, it is likely we shall see little tariff reduction by developing countries. This follows from flexibility in proposed tariff cutting formulas (meaning lesser liberalization criteria for developing countries), combined with the structure of tariff schedules.

Consider Brazil, India, and Thailand as shown in Table 4.1. These countries span the spectrum of developing country bindings. Brazil's tariffs are all bound, though the average rate for industrial products is 14.9 percentage points above the current applied rate. This gap is called a binding overhang (Francois and Martin 2003.). India and Thailand's tariffs are partially covered by bindings, again with a significant binding overhang. In general, for developing countries, the binding overhang is so large that reductions in the range of 50 per cent are necessary to force any reductions at all in average applied rates for countries like Brazil. For many countries, even this will have little or no effect, as tariffs are largely unbound. Moreover, in reality the cuts are likely to be in the range of 24 per cent, yielding very little actual liberalization even for countries like India and Thailand. This is also why the debate over using bound, applied or 'historic' rates in the WTO has been so important as a starting point for negotiations.

Any realistic scenario will yield tariff and subsidy reductions in developed countries, and very little liberalization outside that group of countries. This has very different implications for the distribution of gains from the WTO process. The study underlying Chapter 2 does work with bindings data and applied data, and so presumably the Doha scenario is actually an 'OECD liberalizes' scenario. It would have been useful to see some decomposition of the liberalization in developed and developing countries under the Doha scenario. We need a better understanding of the implications of a system where developing countries never really have to do anything with respect to tariff reductions. We could then gauge the importance of developing countries going in for liberalization, given the context of a system where they probably will not actually do so. Of course, lack of developing country participation limits their negotiating leverage in sectors of interest, which also has implications for the pattern of tariff reductions in developed countries. Witness remaining high tariffs in textiles and clothing.

The importance of agriculture

Studies differ in the emphasis they place on agriculture. We should expect losers from agricultural liberalization. Yet, the full merchandise trade liberalization scenario only has winners. This seems suspicious. Reduction of domestic and export subsidies by the developed countries – the EU and USA in particular – would raise world food prices. Because some developing nations are net food exporters and some net food importers, a narrow focus on rich-nation agricultural liberalization would have mixed effects on the South. The point is that, regardless of how unfair they may be, EU and US subsidies foster terms-of-trade gains for food importers and terms-of-trade losses for food exporters. Moreover, some of the biggest food exporters – Canada, New Zealand, and Australia – are not developing countries. Thus, a narrow focus on agriculture liberalization in developed countries in any realistic scenario will produce substantial gains for rich consumers and food exporters in developed countries, but very uneven gains for developing countries. Yet, in the results reported, there are winners across the board. This may be because the South gains more if the developing and developed countries simultaneously would liberalize their agricultural sectors. This may be the difference between the Doha and global scenarios. In any event, one is left wanting to see some decomposition of the impact of liberalization in developed and developing countries, both in the full liberalization and the Doha scenario.

A message front and centre in this study is that liberalization of agriculture and food yields 62 per cent of total gains. There should be a warning label around this statement. The WTO process covers services, trade and foreign direct investment (FDI). It also covers trade facilitation, and intellectual property rights. These have the potential to far outweigh the impact of reducing trade barriers in food products. It implies that we should not focus on matters that are downplayed simply because they are not included in the model and policy scenarios. This is apart from the issue of market structure and economies of scale. The addition of such factors tends to shift the weight back to manufacturing and services, and away from agriculture, even when we do not focus on trade facilitation and non-market access aspects of the WTO. The result is that we may be driving the policy process to focus on what is in our models, and to ignore what is not.

References

Abreu, M. (1996) 'Trade in Manufactures, the Outcome of the Uruguay Round and Developing Country Interests', in W. Martin and L.A. Winters (eds), *The Uruguay Round and the Developing Countries*, Cambridge: Cambridge University Press.

Bouet, A., Decreux, Y., Fontagne, L., Jean, S., and Laborde, D. (2004) 'A Consistent, Ad-Valorem Equivalent Measure of Applied Protection Across the World: The MAcMap-HS6 database', discussion paper No. 2004-22, December, Paris: CEPII.

Francois, J.F. and Martin, W. (2003) 'Formùla Approaches to Market Access Negotiations', *World Economy*, 26: 1–28.

Francois, J.F., Van Meijl, H., and Van Tongeren, F. (2005) 'Trade Liberalization in the Doha Development Round', *Economic Policy*, 20: 349–391.

UNCTAD (2004) 'Beyond Conventional Wisdom in Development Policy: An Intellectual History of UNCTAD, 1964–2004', UNCTAD/EDM/2004/4.

5 Services and the Doha Development Agenda

Southern perspectives

Pierre Sauvé

Introduction

Long deemed non-tradeable, cross-border trade in services increased by 6 per cent on an average over the last decade and a half, keeping pace with merchandise trade. Throughout this period, several categories of services have ranked among the fastest growing components of the world economy. Total measurable trade in services, as defined by the four types of transactions subject to multilateral disciplines, stood at some 1.8 trillion US dollars at the end of 2003. Developing country service exports accounted for just under a quarter of the total, amounting to some 377 billion US dollars in 2003.

The Doha Development Agenda (DDA) is often presented as a mercantilist bargain between developing country exports of agricultural products and developed country services exports. A closer look at trends in aggregate data suggests otherwise. The gap between developed and developing countries in the share of services in total trade has been closing rapidly. Developing countries have seen their service exports increase by a factor of four during the last decade, faster than exports of goods. In the process, the share of services in total exports reached 24 per cent in 2004. This aggregate performance exceeds the contribution that services make to exports of developed countries, which has hovered steadily around 21–22 per cent in recent years.

The bulk of trade in services takes place via an established presence, that is, via foreign direct investment (FDI), as service suppliers typically need to establish a commercial presence abroad in order to access the market effectively. Not surprisingly, the service sector accounts for almost half of the global stock of FDI and some two-thirds of annual FDI flows have been directed towards service industries in recent years (UNCTAD 2003). More important still from a policy perspective, trade in services takes place where more than four of five barriers to international investment are concentrated (Sauvé *et al.* forthcoming).

Although developed countries dominate global trade and investment in services, developing countries are often specialized in – and dependent on – exports of services as a source of foreign-exchange earnings: 21 developing countries were found in the list of the world's top 40 service exporting nations in 2003, and 5 of them – China, Hong Kong China, India, Korea and Singapore – ranked in the top 10. Services represent a significant source of export earnings even for some of the world's poorest countries. In the 49 countries classified as least-developed countries (LDCs) by the United Nations (UN), the average contribution of services exports to Gross Domestic Product (GDP) was 6.5 per cent in 2001, with some small island LDCs such as Vanuatu and the Maldives reaching (tourism-induced) levels of over 50 per cent (UN 2005).

Services are used intensively in the production of all goods and services, making up around 10–20 per cent of production costs in manufacturing and agriculture, and sometimes more (an estimated 20–25 per cent in some countries' ready-made garments industry; UN 2005). Much of what is required to trade – telecommunications, transport, banking and insurance, logistics, distribution – consists of services. The earlier quoted figures and observations attest to the economic and commercial significance of the services sector and of negotiations aimed at progressively rolling back impediments to trade and investment in it.

Long hesitant to commit significantly to market opening in services, a growing number of developing countries are today active *demandeurs* in the World Trade Organization (WTO) and regional negotiations. This is especially true in areas where they have strong comparative advantages, such as in tourism, construction, computer, shipping and many labour-based services as illustrated in Box 5.1. To some extent, such a trend also reflects the strong recent increase in trade in services among developing countries in sectors as diverse as audio–visual, maritime transport, health, telecommunications and a host of business services (OECD 2003).

Negotiations under the General Agreement on Trade in Services (GATS) resumed in January 2000 as part of the Uruguay Round's built-in agenda. The talks have subsequently been integrated into the DDA and are subject to the same deadlines as all other areas under negotiation. This chapter explores prospects for securing a development-friendly outcome of the negotiations on services in the DDA.

A development-friendly set of multilateral disciplines

Due to its voluntary, 'bottom-up', approach to liberalization, the GATS allows WTO members to select the sectors, modes of supply and regulatory

Box 5.1 Moving upscale: exporting services through outsourcing

Technological advances in telecommunication and computer industries have allowed developing countries endowed with a well-educated and costs-competitive workforce to compete successfully in the world market for computer-related services. While the remarkable performance of the Indian software industry is perhaps the most celebrated case, such export success is hardly confined to South Asia.

By helping overcome hurdles of time, space and size, services supplied over electronic networks afford developing country firms the means to integrate into global markets. Outsourcing and back-office operations, covering computer and related business as well as professional, financial or audio-visual services, have become key areas of export interest for developing countries.

Outsourcing can both leverage and help to support existing service exports, as in the audio-visual sector, where countries with large film and broadcasting industries, such as India, Brazil or Mexico, are also increasingly moving into outsourced post-production for other films.

To reap such benefits, developing countries will need modern, efficient infrastructure, especially in telecommunications, solid educational systems (with a premium placed on the acquisition of language skills), as well as the means to supply developed country markets services on a cross-border basis. Meanwhile, care must be taken that policies in developed countries support such trends by resisting calls for erecting new barriers for fear of white-collar job displacement.

Source: OECD (2003) *Services Liberalisation: Identifying Opportunities and Gains – Key Findings*, Paris: OECD, Working Party of the Trade Committee.

conditions in which commitments to open markets are made. Such flexibility and the emphasis in GATS on the progressive nature of liberalization help explain why the agreement is often described as the most 'development-friendly' of all Uruguay Round agreements (OECD 2002a). Indeed, the GATS is unique in the freedom it affords member countries in integrating the multilateral trading system at their own pace and in accordance with their national priorities and objectives. The agreement establishes a series of means through which countries can limit, condition or even suspend the commitments they make.

The relative novelty and overall complexity of trade in services resulted in a limited initial harvest of liberalization commitments in the Uruguay Round.[1] Most attention was focused on the development of a yet unfinished framework of rules governing the progressive liberalization of services markets. Outstanding rule-making negotiations under GATS are proceeding in four areas: emergency safeguards, domestic regulation, subsidies and government procurement of services. The limited liberalization commitments of the initial WTO members under the GATS shows that these countries have enjoyed considerable policy flexibility, with the notable exception of some newly-acceding countries, which had levels of initial commitments that were higher than the levels of commitments of developed countries in the Uruguay Round.

Several of the GATS provisions focus specifically on the particular needs and constraints faced by developing countries in services trade. For instance, the Agreement's preamble recalls the particular need developing countries may have to regulate their services markets in accordance with national policy objectives. Article IV, Increasing Participation of Developing Countries, focuses attention on the practical means of enhancing the participation of developing countries in world trade in services, notably through improved access to information networks and distribution channels.

Similarly, Article XIX, Negotiation of Specific Commitments, on which the modalities governing the current set of multilateral negotiations are based, provides that there shall be appropriate flexibility for developing countries, and especially LDCs, to open fewer sectors, liberalize fewer types of transactions, extend market access in line with their development situation and attach conditions aimed at strengthening their domestic services capacity and competitiveness.

Crucially, the GATS calls on developed countries to lift restrictions in sectors and modes of supply of export interest to developing countries. Such calls were re-emphasized in the Doha Work Programme (DWP) for services that WTO members reaffirmed in the July 2004 decision of the trade body's General Council, as shown in Annex 5.1.

Developing countries rightfully complain that little has been done to date to meet the above challenges. Finding the appropriate means of doing so will be an important litmus test of the DDA if it is to fulfil its stated development promise.

What can WTO engagement help achieve in services?

In marked contrast to agriculture, services negotiations in the DDA take place against a backdrop of far-reaching recent trade and investment liberalization, much of it unilaterally decreed. The two sectors thus confront starkly different negotiating environments. In agriculture, negotiations are crucial in driving even the most modest reforms. In services, multilateral and regional negotiations essentially play a complementary role, affording countries periodic opportunities to lock in the domestic policy they are prone to pursue between negotiating rounds. While such political economy underpinnings imply that the DDA could generate significant gains simply by harvesting existing levels of market openness in services markets, it also points to a real dilemma: whether and how to push for a grand bargain on services if market opening is already occurring unilaterally? Simply put, what incentives can be found to translate ongoing liberalization into WTO commitments?

A DDA bargain on services is worth pursuing for at least two main reasons. First, unilateral liberalization, while genuine and widespread, is far from even across regions, countries, sectors and modes of supply. Prohibitive barriers remain, particularly in areas of particular interest to developing countries such as the movement of service suppliers. Second, in the mercantilist world of trade negotiations, the willingness of developing countries to lock in recent service sector reforms by GATS commitments can afford them leverage to push more credibly for necessary technical and financial assistance, as argued later, to implement service-sector commitments, or for commitments from trading partners in other priority areas of the DDA. To put it differently, services negotiations offer developing countries the opportunity to act in their own economic interest and be paid for it at the negotiating table (UN 2005).

Governments at all levels of development face the difficult task of designing services reforms to generate sustainable gains in overall economic performance while minimizing adjustment costs to avoid social hardship and promoting pro-poor outcomes in terms of access to essential services. While achieving successful outcomes remains, first and foremost, a domestic policy challenge, engagement in multilateral services negotiations can nonetheless help support domestic policy reform efforts. It can do so in five distinct manners.

First, reciprocity-based bargaining can help governments overcome domestic opposition to reform. Pursuit of reforms and further liberalization can be easier to implement if a government can demonstrate that its exporters will gain from improved market access negotiated in other areas of a WTO round. As most developing countries have fewer internationally competitive service sectors than developed countries have, this may limit reciprocal bargaining within services under the GATS. The WTO offers scope for cross-sectional trade-offs – which will likely be necessary to ensure an 'equitable' exchange of market access concessions.

Second, domestic reforms cannot address barriers in foreign markets. The only feasible means of doing so is by pursuing reciprocal liberalization opportunities with key trading partners.

Third, a multilateral commitment that is binding under international law and therefore more difficult (and costly) to reverse in the future, can strengthen the credibility of domestic policies, contributing to an improved investment climate. Locking in current policy under international law or progressively closing the gap between existing policies and international commitments, can send a potentially powerful signal to investors that a government is committed to opening its services markets and to safeguarding such openness. The credibility-enhancing properties of multilateral commitments rank among the most important features of the GATS and of rule-making in the WTO generally.

Fourth, the GATS framework offers the possibility of pre-committing to future liberalization with a view to instilling a greater sense of urgency to needed domestic regulatory reforms whilst promoting orderly adjustment. A scheduled commitment to future liberalization may be more credible than a purely domestic reform announcement, particularly in countries saddled with higher risk premiums. Under such circumstances, all stakeholders in a given sector face a clear, irrevocable, deadline to prepare for a reformed policy environment.[2]

Fifth, additional commitments on transparency and regulatory principles can be important complements to the removal of explicit barriers to trade in services under the GATS. Such disciplines assure foreign traders and investors that liberal market access commitments will not be nullified or impaired by the imposition of regulatory barriers to trade in services or the non-transparent and discretionary implementation of regulations such as the allocation of licenses. In addition, commitment to multilaterally agreed principles on transparency and domestic regulation can help promote the adoption of 'best practice' or 'pro-competitive' regulation at home, as has happened in the telecommunications sector (Mattoo and Sauvé 2003).

A development agenda for services

Addressing a deficit in readiness to negotiate

As noted earlier, services negotiations resumed in January 2000 as part of the Uruguay Round's built-in agenda, alongside negotiations on agriculture to which they are inevitably, albeit only indirectly, linked. A large number of developing countries have encountered difficulties in identifying their specific sectoral interests in the current negotiations, the barriers to their exports or the impact of detailed requests by developed countries on their services sectors. Not surprisingly, progress in tabling meaningful liberalization commitments has been slow, with several leading service exporters among the developing countries having yet to submit their initial offers. Also, some countries advanced proposals that fail singularly to lock in the regulatory *status quo*, partly on tactical grounds given the perception of stalled progress under other negotiating chapters of the DDA.

Of particular concern to developing countries is the question of how to evaluate the requests received from trading partners and the formulation of their own requests and offers. The latter is a particularly complex task as countries need to determine their national policy objectives and the competitiveness of each (sub) sector. Such challenges are compounded by the need to determine the optimal sequencing of the steps involved in liberalization, the capacity of domestic firms to provide the services in question and to determine whether this capacity would be positively or negatively affected by further competition in the market, as well as the adequacy of domestic regulatory regimes and enforcement capacities. Other elements of such an evaluation relate to the impact of market opening on investment, employment and access to higher quality imports or more efficient foreign suppliers.

Addressing the clear deficit in negotiating capacities that most developing countries face under the GATS requires that a fresh look be given in the DDA to the idea of linking scheduled commitments, now or in future, to legally binding provisions on the provision of needed technical assistance aimed at strengthening the negotiating and supply capacities of developing countries. This issue is taken up later.

Achieving progress on Modes 1 and 4: the twin challenges of labour mobility and outsourcing

Developing countries enjoy a clear comparative advantage in labour-intensive services, including higher-skilled services in a growing number of areas. Service supply via temporary movement of service suppliers (Mode 4) is thus a key priority for the GATS negotiations. But increasingly so too is the supply of labour-intensive services by Mode 1 involving cross-border or remote supply in the form of international outsourcing of computer and business process services. Both Mode 4 and outsourcing promise real export gains for developing countries. In both cases, a growing volume of trade is already underway. The question for the DDA is to see how best to translate this reality into GATS commitments and to use the negotiations to head off actual or potential obstacles to future growth.

While long seen as essentially substitutable, services supplied under both modes are increasingly complementary for many of the types of business activities that are outsourced. However, Mode 4 commitments remain extremely limited. Constraints on the cross-border movement of service suppliers are among the most important existing asymmetries in commitments under the GATS and need to be addressed by specific openings by developed countries, starting in the DDA.

In the context of securing increased Mode 1 commitments from developed countries, or at least a locking in of what are currently generally favourable market-access conditions, developing countries are seeking to gain parallel Mode 4 openings needed to supply services related to these activities.

More complex, higher value-added activities tend to involve the temporary movement of natural persons during the preparatory and follow up phases, even though the final services may be provided through cross-border supply. Such linkages imply changes in the need for movement of natural persons, such that as countries move up to higher value outsourcing and business process outsourcing activities, the need for mobility of natural persons will not diminish but rather shift towards higher level service providers.

Mode 1 trade depends crucially on the availability, quality and cost-effectiveness of telecommunications services as the basic infrastructure for cross-border trade. Computer-based and related services are also enabling services for cross-border trade in many other service sectors. Liberalization of these particular services could therefore act as catalysts in making them more accessible to end-users and in promoting trade through Mode 1 in other relevant service sectors of export interest to developing countries. This explains why a number of developing countries are seeking progress in liberalization of computer-based and related services as a necessary pre-condition for enhancing Mode 1 trade across all service sectors, and for outsourcing. Developed countries are also being asked to undertake enhanced commitments on various categories of professionals in the area of computer-related services. In this regard, numerical restrictions on the entry of professionals in foreign markets for the supply of services would need to be removed, and more provision made for mobility of these professionals through the issuance of temporary entry visas.

Multilateral liberalization of trade in services through Mode 4 constitutes a key unfinished development agenda of the Uruguay Round. It is also an essential element of a balanced and development-orientated outcome of the current negotiations. Multilateral liberalization of Mode 4 must be buttressed by a reduction and streamlining of market-entry conditions if substantive development gains are to be assured by the international trading system.

Movement of natural persons supplying services extends beyond short-term economic, trade and competitiveness benefits for developing countries. By providing employment opportunities abroad on a temporary basis, it can be an effective tool in addressing unemployment in the domestic (sending country) economy, thereby contributing directly to poverty reduction.

Workers' repatriated earnings in the form of remittances transferred to their home countries are an important way of generating investment and savings, and promoting accelerated development of the domestic economy. Remittances have in recent years emerged as one of the most stable, continuous and counter-cyclical sources of development finance. For many countries, particularly LDCs, such flows dwarf FDI and aid as a source of external funding. Moreover, as workers return to their home countries after temporary employment as service providers abroad, the entrepreneurship and knowledge acquired abroad can stimulate the growth of domestic service sectors and enhance sending countries' ability to assimilate and apply new technologies.

An important – if always daunting – challenge in the Doha Round is to attempt to separate Mode 4 trade – of a temporary character – from immigration-related matters so as to mitigate the difficult and often emotive political and cultural issues that can hamper realization of the full benefits of facilitated temporary entry for home and host countries alike. It is generally believed that liberalized, but regulated, movement of temporary workers could help to attenuate problems of clandestine and illegal migration.

While developing countries are pinning high hopes on Mode 4 liberalization in the DDA, it is essential that expectations be kept rational. Mode 4 liberalization faces three daunting challenges. A first challenge stems from the inherently cyclical nature of labour markets, and the corresponding reluctance of labour market and immigration officials to take on quasi-permanent legal commitments in a trade-policy setting. A second challenge arises from the obligation under GATS to extend liberalization commitments on a most-favoured nation (MFN) basis, a privilege many WTO members may be reluctant to bestow on foreign workers, particularly in low- to medium-skilled categories. A third challenge, alluded to earlier, owes to the inherent difficulty of separating the trade from the non-trade components in immigration policy. While trade is an important driver of labour mobility, it is by no means the only one, nor always the most important one. Seeking to pigeon hole temporary access to labour markets in a multilateral trade-policy setting, and to address those worker categories whose enhanced temporary mobility would make the greatest impact on poverty reduction, is thus far from easy. Such progress may be more feasible – and the downsides more easily contained – under bilateral (guest-worker) or plurilateral labour market agreements than in the WTO.

Still, while obstacles to a bigger bargain on Mode 4 are significant, there is undeniable scope for progress in the DDA and in subsequent WTO negotiating rounds, not least because the underlying forces – population aging and acute labour shortages in certain occupational categories in developed countries, and a growing supply of workers in all skill categories from developing countries – are not about to abate. A development-friendly outcome on Mode 4 in the Doha Round would include the following elements:

i   broadening the categories of service providers eligible for temporary entry to include independent workers and contractual service providers;

ii   including some lower-skilled levels and occupations, notably in areas such as construction, agriculture and personal care services;
iii eliminating economic needs tests or reducing their incidence by making them more predictable through establishment of common transparent criteria;
iv   simplifying, streamlining and easing the granting of temporary entry visas, work permits and licensing requirements and procedures;
v   facilitating the recognition of professional qualifications, including through mutual recognition agreements and horizontal application of the GATS guidelines on accountancy to other regulated professions.

As far as Mode 1 commitments on outsourcing-related activities are concerned, the main challenge developing countries face is that of maintaining the currently benign trading environment for servicing foreign markets through remote supply. Such trade is today largely market-driven and relatively free of restrictions, a state of affairs that the DDA could usefully lock in to the benefit of developing country exporters. As outsourcing has grown, so too have concerns about the export of white-collar jobs to developing countries. Such arguments exert undeniable political traction in many parts of the developed world, prompting a number of legislatures to enact measures aimed at preventing offshore companies from bidding for government procurement contracts or exploring fiscal disincentives for offshoring various services functions.

Two issues need to be addressed in the DDA in pursuing a development-friendly Mode 1 agenda. First, WTO Members will need to map the universe of service transactions covered by outsourcing-related activities for purposes of scheduling future liberalization commitments. This will entail reaching agreement on the definition and classification of activities that did not exist at the time of the Uruguay Round. Second, WTO Members should decide whether they might usefully apply Article XVIII, Additional Commitments, and undertake not to introduce new barriers, including of a government-procurement nature, that inhibit the cross-border supply of covered outsourced-related services in which specific commitments are made.

Liberalizing FDI in infrastructure services

The strong contribution that key enabling services can make to overall economic performance means that developing countries have much to gain from scheduling deeper commitments on Mode 3 trade, commercial presence or FDI in services, particularly in a number of key infrastructural services such as telecommunications, finance, energy and transport. Barriers to investment in these sectors are often among the highest in developing countries. Mode 3 imports can form the basis for developing an export capacity in a number of professional, financial, transportation or even health and education services.

While promising significant potential gains, negotiations in infrastructural services can represent important challenges. The social dimension of many services and the universal provision of essential services such as health, education, transport, telecommunications and cultural services raise a dilemma inasmuch as the need arises to reconcile a complex set of non-economic objectives with efficiency and international competitiveness. It is increasingly recognized that developing countries should condition liberalization in these areas on the existence of appropriate safety nets and regulatory institutions to ensure that liberalizing reforms will prove beneficial and politically sustainable. One way of addressing such challenges consists of pre-committing to future market opening and to possibly link such commitments to demands for the provision of assistance for the development of adequate regulatory frameworks and the strengthening of supply capacities.

Developing countries including LDCs are increasingly aware of the need to attach specific conditions to their market-access offers in terms of new investment and technology transfer requirements that may improve the supply capacity and competitiveness of their services sectors. The formulation of appropriate conditions that could be attached to their new schedules of commitments needs to take into account issues such as:

i   the unique situation of each country as regards the pace and path of liberalization most suitable to domestic circumstances;

ii   the need for flexibility in addressing problems that cannot be anticipated when undertaking liberalization commitments;

iii the lack of meaningful concessions, critical barriers to exports and supply constraints preventing developing countries from reaping benefits;

iv   the fact that benefits from privatization and liberalization do not accrue automatically but require certain preconditions, including an appropriate regulatory framework, entrepreneurial and technological capacity building and complementary policies; and

v   adjustment costs, including those entailed by the need to ensure access to universal and essential services, in particular for the most vulnerable segments of the population.

The importance of domestic regulation

Other important issues in the current GATS negotiations relate to the effective implementation of Article IV, Increasing Participation of Developing Countries, and Article XIX.2, Negotiation of Specific Commitments, and would require two operational elements: facilitation of exports, that is, enhanced, non-reciprocal access to developed country markets for developing-country exports, and flexibility and policy discretion regarding developing countries' approach to their own markets, that is, the right to regulate and pursue developmental objectives, maintain some trade and investment barriers and provide appropriate support to domestic services providers.

A closely related area in the services negotiations relates to Article VI.4, Domestic Regulation, particularly in respect of the right of members to regulate, and to introduce new regulations, governing the supply of services within their territories in order to meet national policy objectives. Given existing asymmetries with respect to the degree of development of services regulations in different countries, the particular need of developing countries to exercise this right has been recognized in the preamble of the GATS. Accordingly, Para. 7 of the Doha Ministerial Declaration reaffirms the right to regulate and to introduce new regulations governing the supply of services.

Regulatory reform is of key importance to developing countries, and many of them have repeatedly emphasized that a country's planned pace of liberalization needs to be adjusted so that its supervisory and regulatory capabilities are not compromised. Difficulties in this area stem from several factors, not least of which relates to the social impact of domestic regulations, particularly in sectors featuring public good characteristics and where the provision of universal services is deemed essential. There is a need to develop clear Special and Differential Treatment (SDT) provisions in any future disciplines on domestic regulation.

Of particular concern are issues relating to flexibility to engage in regulatory reforms, pursue various public policy objectives and seek to guarantee universal access to key services. Of all the unfinished rule-making issues confronting the services community, domestic regulation is arguably that where development-friendly negotiating advances are most likely. This is not to say that rule-making discussions on emergency safeguard measures, subsidies or government procurement lack in importance, but is rather a recognition that these issues currently show few signs of commanding consensus-based decisions under the DDA.

Formula-based negotiations and the interests of the LDCs

Several voices have been heard expressing alarm at the lack of engagement of WTO members in the DDA services negotiations. There are doubtless several reasons for this, starting with the generally desultory progress registered elsewhere in the negotiations, particularly in agriculture, which is by all accounts the defining issue of the DDA. The 'agriculture comes first' aspect of the DDA has quite naturally relegated services to a secondary role, with many leading developing countries – those with arguably most at stake in services and in the DDA more generally – holding back until developed countries show and play their cards in farm trade.

Still, it would be a mistake to read too much into such an account of the current state of play of DDA talks in services, as cross-sectoral considerations tend to weigh more heavily in negotiating bargains towards the very end of multilateral negotiations. Faced with an outstanding rule-making agenda on services that shows little signs of DDA-induced progress, a number of proposals have been made to impart momentum to the market-access dimension of negotiations under the GATS. To this end, several formulas have been proposed, for the most part by developed countries that are quite naturally the most vocal *demandeurs* at the negotiating table.

Most formulas centre on the idea of ratcheting up the overall level of bound commitments under GATS. The simplest approach would be to define a percentage of service sectors to be covered by binding commitments and/or the number of sectors subject to full market opening that is, with no restrictions on national treatment and market access. While such an approach can be deemed attractive, one can easily see how it could translate into commitments in sectors that are less commercially meaningful for the sake of meeting a quantitative threshold. A more promising, but arguably less politically attractive alternative, would be for WTO members to strive to lock in the regulatory *status quo* in sectors in which they voluntarily choose to schedule commitments. Doing so would reduce what in some instances are significant gaps between the actual level of market access afforded under domestic laws and regulations, and the lower level of access provided under existing GATS commitments. The decision to allow WTO members to schedule commitments below the *status quo* was taken in the Uruguay Round, replicating in services the mercantilist instincts long practiced in the negotiations on tariffs for manufactured goods. In the Uruguay Round, only developing countries availed themselves of such flexibility, as the norm for developed countries was to lock in the prevailing level of market openness in their GATS schedules. While closing the gap between applied and bound regulation would increase the predictability and transparency of host countries' services regimes, contributing in the process to enhancing the investment climate, it bears noting that most developing countries appear unwilling to break with past practice.

The DWP for services usefully calls for a review to be undertaken prior to the conclusion of the DDA to assess the degree to which WTO members have complied with their pledge to schedule commitments in sectors and modes of supply of priority interest to developing countries. See Annex 5.1 for the DWP for services. Such a review will likely exert meaningful and much needed political pressure on developed countries to live up to their promises of placing development at the heart of the current negotiating round.

While it is generally understood that a development round will place few if any demands for market opening on the part of the LDCs, there is, in services as in all other facets of the DDA, a marked contrast between the handful of developing country players who stand to reap a large share of the benefits that the DDA may yet generate under the GATS, and the majority of developing countries with limited export interests in services trade, weak regulatory institutions and acute resource constraints. For the latter group of countries, harnessing the reciprocal benefits of market opening under GATS is simply not a realistic proposition. This is so not because services are unimportant, which they clearly are, but because the WTO negotiations cannot be expected to deliver much by way of a development bargain in the service sectors that matter most to them – tourism or movement of lower-skilled labour. Moreover, for countries with limited export capacity in services, the mercantilist and export-driven request-offer process on which GATS negotiations are based lessens the incentive to schedule commitments (typically on the import side, such as Mode 3) that are likely to exert a beneficial impact on economy-wide performance. The most likely end result may thus be a continuation of the dual trends of unilateral disarmament alongside limited engagement under GATS for a large part of the WTO membership.

Trade-Related Technical Assistance and capacity building

The DDA is full of references to trade-related capacity building, none of which however are legally binding. To guard against the real risk that the absence of technical assistance may stymie needed reforms and unduly hold back development-enhancing liberalization commitments, consideration should be given to establishing a more formal link between enhanced market-access commitments by developing countries and additional assistance on the part of developed countries. Such a link could lend more credibility to liberalization and programmes for technical assistance.

The question arises where additional assistance should be directed to. Developing countries face two central challenges in undertaking service sector reforms. First, identifying the elements of an economically sound services policy. Second, assessing how the choice of a sound policy at the domestic level can be supported by multilateral or regional negotiations. Many developing countries are at a distinct disadvantage in meeting such challenges (OECD 2002b). There is much that properly targeted

Trade-Related Technical Assistance and the strengthening of institutional and regulatory capacities can do to help harness the full potential of reforms of the service sector.

WTO members cannot participate meaningfully in services negotiations without first understanding how domestic reform is best pursued. This requires careful analysis informed by dialogue between national stakeholders, country negotiators and independent researchers. A stocktaking exercise to consider national and cross-country experience with reform of the service sector could help identify areas where reforms can be fast-tracked and areas where uncertainties suggest more regulatory precaution. An assessment of the effects of services liberalization is foreseen under GATS. The donor community could lend credibility to such an assessment by setting up a group of internationally recognized experts to lead and direct such work. An initiative of this type could help ensure that WTO commitments reflect sound economic policy rather than the dictates of domestic or foreign pressure groups (Mattoo 2003).

Much of the effort to capacity building in services has so far focused on helping negotiators and policy officials master the legal provisions of the GATS. A more pressing need, and one that is arguably more conducive to harnessing the pro-development potential of the GATS, is that of acquiring the analytical tools to determine a country's readiness to liberalize; develop government-wide negotiating strategies; and help domestic service providers take full advantage of the market-access opportunities arising from regional and multilateral liberalization efforts.

Technical assistance directed to the earlier needs deserves more attention on the part of multilateral agencies and the donor community. Largely, this entails the dissemination of knowledge on best-practice initiatives in countries that have been successful reformers. Invariably, these countries will have developed efficient communication channels with the multiplicity of stakeholders that services negotiations entail.

Another area where technical assistance can make a difference concerns the strengthening of regulatory agencies. Regulatory institutions can be costly and require staff with sophisticated legal and economic skills. Yet sound domestic regulation is critical to realizing the full benefits of open service markets and responding to their potential downsides.

Helping developing countries improve domestic standards and qualifications for services, notably by strengthening their participation in regional or global standard-setting initiatives, is another area where more focused capacity building efforts can yield strong development dividends. Low standards and related inadequacies in domestic regulation can frustrate access of developing country services and service providers to foreign markets. They can also legitimize existing trade and investment barriers directed against such exports.

Finally, enhanced assistance may be related to designing reforms that properly factor the impact of liberalization on the poor and improve their access to essential services. Such services run the gamut from sanitation to transport, telecommunications, small-scale finance, education and health. While most of these complimentary policy challenges are outside the realm of GATS negotiations, getting them right can help build needed support for reform efforts. However, implementing such policies in an economically sound manner can present numerous challenges to weak bureaucracies, and many developing countries, particularly LDCs, will require outside support in meeting them.

Concluding remarks

The DDA provides an opportunity to achieve commercially meaningful market-access commitments in sectors and modes of interest to developing countries, particularly labour-intensive services, and to devise effective benchmarks for the implementation of Article IV, Increasing Participation of Developing Countries. However, for many developing countries, priority areas remain the proper sequencing of service sector reform, tackling acute supply constraints, identifying of national policy objectives, and capacity building even more than market access. Actions by developed countries to grant market access and support investment and technology flows in key services sectors of developing countries will play a determining role in ensuring a pro-development outcome in services negotiations.

In order to maximize the development benefits from liberalization of trade in services, the focus needs to be on strengthening the ability of governments to implement effective and pro-poor regulatory frameworks. Addressing service sector issues needs to be grounded in an understanding of the role of services both as essential to the well-being of people and as key production inputs, their current domestic availability and the existing range of service exports. This means, *inter alia*, ensuring that liberalization and development assistance for essential services, that is, water, health and education, is not leading to the adoption of a particular economic model, such as privatization, but gives necessary attention to domestic regulatory reform and the expression of local collective preferences. Also, this would imply that low-costs access to essential services, including high-speed telecommunications infrastructure and the internet, is readily available in rural communities, and that there be no restrictions on the ability to cross-subsidize the provision of services to rural areas. Moreover, measures are required to increase lending to small and medium-sized enterprises and poor producers, and to avoid that initiatives directed at attracting FDI crowd out local service suppliers.

Moreover, substantial benefits could be derived from liberalization of restrictive measures hampering the ability of workers from developing countries to take jobs in developed countries on a temporary basis and to supply markets remotely on a cross-border basis without undue restraints. Hence, market access for services of export interest to developing countries, particularly under Modes 1 and 4, should be liberalized on a priority basis.

The Uruguay Round and its immediate aftermath focused on services in which developed countries were more competitive: financial services, telecommunications, and professional services, and concentrated on modes of delivery of services other than modes that require the movement of people, except those categories of workers deemed of interest to developed country exporters. By contrast, developing countries have tremendous advantages in unskilled and semi-skilled services, which need to be exploited more fully. Similarly, the comparative advantage that some of them have in off-shore, internet-based, services needs to be sheltered from restrictive measures aimed at retaining jobs in developed countries.

Annex 5.1 The July 2004 Doha work programme for services

Offers: Members who have not submitted offers must do so as soon as possible and revised offers should be tabled by May 2005. Members should strive to ensure a high quality of offers, particularly in sectors and modes of supply of export interest to developing countries, with special attention to LDCs.

Liberalization: Members shall aim to achieve progressively higher levels of liberalization with no a priori exclusion of any service sector or mode of supply and shall give special attention to sectors and modes of supply of export interest to developing countries. Members shall note the interest of developing countries, as well as other Members, in Mode 4.

Rules: Members must intensify their efforts to conclude rules negotiations in accordance with the respective mandates and deadlines.

Technical assistance: Targeted technical assistance should be provided to enable developing countries to participate effectively in the negotiations.

Review: For the purposes of the Sixth Ministerial Meeting, Members shall review progress in the negotiations and make a report to the Trade Negotiations Committee, including possible recommendations.

Source: 'The 2004 DWP Framework', Annex C, WTO Document WT/L/579, 2 August 2004; WTO (2002) *Annual Report 2002*, Geneva: WTO.

Acknowledgement

The author is grateful to Americo Beviglia-Zampetti for helpful comments and discussions.

Notes

1 An indication of the work that lies ahead for securing more meaningful market-access commitments may be gleaned from a calculation of the share of commitments where no restrictions are maintained on market access and national treatment. For developed countries, the share is about 25 per cent of all services, for other members less than 10 per cent (Hoekman and Mattoo 2000).

2 With the exception of a significant number of pre-commitments in the 1996 Agreement on Basic Telecommunications, WTO members have so far not made extensive use of pre-commitments under the GATS. It is widely expected, however, that such a practice will become more widespread in the future for countries that seek to engage more resolutely in the negotiations but may still be unwilling or unable to liberalize fully or immediately.

Bibliography

Chanda, R. (2002) 'GATS and its implications for developing countries: key issues and concern', DESA Discussion Paper, No. 25, New York: United Nations.

Hoekman, B. and Mattoo, A. (2000) 'Services, economic development and the next round of negotiations on services', *Journal of International Development*, 12: 283–296.

ICTSD-IISD (2003) 'Trade in Services', Doha Round Briefing Series: Cancun Update, Volume 2, 13 August, Geneva: International Centre for Trade and Sustainable Development and Winnipeg: International Institute for Sustainable Development.

Mattoo, A. (2003) 'Services in a development round', in The World Trade Brief, London: Agenda Publishing.

Mattoo, A. and Sauvé, P. (eds) (2003) *Domestic Regulation and Services Trade Liberalization*, Washington, DC: Oxford University Press for The World Bank.

Mattoo, A., Rathindran, R. and Subramanian, A. (2001) 'Measuring services trade liberalization and its impact on economic growth: an illustration', The World Bank Policy Research Working Paper, No. 2380, Washington, DC: The World Bank.

OECD (2002a) *GATS: The Case for Open Services Markets*, Paris: OECD.

OECD (2002b) *Managing the Request Offer Process Under GATS*, Paris: OECD.

OECD (2003) *Services Liberalisation: Identifying Opportunities and Gains – Key Findings*, Paris: OECD, Working Party of the Trade Committee.

Sauvé, P. (2002) 'Collective action scenarios on investment', background paper prepared for Global Economic Prospects and the Developing Economies 2003, mimeo, Washington, DC: The World Bank.

Sauvé, P. (2004) 'At the service of development? The GATS and developing countries', Trade Policy Brief No. 4, Stockholm: Swedish International Development Agency. Available online at www.sida.se

Sauvé, P., Molinievo, M. and Tuerk, E. (forthcoming), 'Revealed policy preferences in selected international investment agreements', Investment Issues Series, Geneva: UNCTAD.

UN (2005) *Trade for Development*, A Background Report prepared for the UN Millennium Project, New York: United Nations. Available online at www.unmillenniumproject.org

UNCTAD (2003) *World Investment Report 2003*, Geneva: United Nations.

World Bank, The (2001) *Global Economic Prospects and the Developing Economies 2002*, Washington, DC: The World Bank.

World Bank, The (2003) *Global Economic Prospects and the Developing Economies 2004*, Washington, DC: The World Bank.

WTO (2001) *GATS Fact and Fiction*, Geneva: WTO.

6 Improving Special and Differential Treatment

Some proposals

Bernard Hoekman, Constantine Michalopoulos and L. Alan Winters

Introduction

This chapter discusses options to strengthen the development relevance of the World Trade Organization (WTO).[1] Our premise is that recasting Special and Differential Treatment (SDT) is critical for the relevance of the WTO from a development perspective, and may also be important for the long-term viability of the institution. Cancun strengthened this perception in our minds: the inability to agree on SDT worsened an already bad atmosphere, while the lack of an effective SDT mechanism impeded progress on both the Singapore Issues and merchandise trade – reflecting perceptions on the part of many developed countries that there might be little reciprocal reduction in access barriers and a fear on the part of recipients of preferences that these would be eroded.

Arguments for SDT reform

International trade is important for development and poverty alleviation. It helps raise and sustain growth, a fundamental requirement for reducing poverty, by giving firms and households access to world markets for goods, services and knowledge, lowering prices and increasing the quality and variety of consumption goods, as well as fostering the specialization of economic activity into areas where countries have a comparative advantage (Bhagwati 1988; Irwin 2001). The primary determinant of the benefits from trade is a country's own policies. Establishing the appropriate trade and complementary policies should consequently figure in the design of national development and poverty-reduction strategies. Trade is not a panacea for economic development or for poverty reduction. To benefit from trade liberalization and to safeguard the interests of poor and vulnerable households a supportive investment climate and social safety nets are critical, to mention just two complementary policy areas.

To an increasing extent, countries' trade policies are subject to multilateral and regional disciplines. Moreover, the trade performance of countries is affected by what other countries do. Measures that restrict market access for developing countries' exports goods and services and that lower (raise) the prices of their exports (imports) have direct negative effects on investment incentives and the growth potential of their economies. For example, agricultural support policies – high rates of subsidization and trade barriers – by developed countries increase world price volatility, lock developing countries out of major markets and can lead to import surges that have highly detrimental effects on developing country farmers. Such policies have become a major political barrier to further trade policy reform in developing countries.

The WTO is a forum both to negotiate improved market access and to agree to 'rules of the game' for trade-related policies. Developing countries gain from both dimensions. A rules-based world trading system is beneficial to developing countries as they are mostly small players on world markets with little ability to influence the policies of large countries. The rules of the WTO can also be beneficial by reducing uncertainty regarding the policies that will be applied by governments – thus potentially helping to increase domestic investment and reduce risks.

Much depends, however, on getting the rules 'right'. To a significant extent WTO rules reflect the interests of rich countries: they are less demanding about distortionary policies that are favoured by these countries and they largely mirror the 'best practice' disciplines that have over time been put in place by them. Thus, the substantial latitude that exists in the WTO for the use of agricultural subsidization reflects the use of such support policies in many developed countries. The same is true of the permissive approach that has historically been taken towards the use of import quotas on textiles – which in principle was prohibited by General Agreement on Tariffs and Trade (GATT) rules. More recently, the inclusion of rules on the protection of intellectual property rights has led to the perception that the WTO contract continues to be unbalanced.[2]

Ensuring that the rules are supportive of development and are seen to be so by the majority of stakeholders in society is perhaps the most fundamental challenge confronting the WTO from a development point of view. Traditionally, developing countries have sought 'differential and more favourable treatment' in the GATT/WTO with a view to increasing the development relevance of the trading system (Finger 1991; Hudec 1987; Michalopoulos 2000). Such SDT was made a permanent element of the trading system in 1979 through the Enabling Clause (formally: Differential and More Favourable Treatment, Reciprocity and Fuller Participation of Developing Countries). This calls for preferential market access for developing countries, limits reciprocity in negotiating rounds to levels 'consistent with development needs' and provides developing countries with greater freedom to use trade policies than would otherwise be permitted by GATT rules.

The Doha Ministerial Declaration reaffirmed the importance of SDT by stating that 'provisions for Special and Differential Treatment are an integral part of the WTO agreements'. It called for a review of WTO SDT provisions with the objective of 'strengthening them and making them more precise, effective and operational' (Para. 44). The Declaration also states that 'modalities for further commitments, including provisions for Special and Differential Treatment, be established no later than 31 March 2003' (Para. 14). Efforts during 2002 to come to agreement on ways to strengthen and operationalize SDT provisions were not successful. Indeed, it became apparent that there are deep divisions between WTO members on the appropriate scope of SDT and how to improve SDT provisions.[3] Many developing countries regard SDT provisions as being meaningless, while many developed countries regard them as bad economics and outdated.

Proposals for reform

There are currently two major dimensions of SDT in the WTO: market access and rules. On market access, SDT involves a call for preferential access for developing countries to markets of developed countries, complemented by less than full reciprocity in negotiating rounds. On rules, SDT includes calls for developed countries to provide technical assistance to low-income countries to help them implement disciplines, complemented with exemptions from certain WTO rules. Such exemptions may be transitory, and involve longer time periods for implementation. This is the case, for example, for the rules on customs valuation, the requirement to abolish Trade-Related Investment Measures (TRIMS), and the implementation of harmonized protection of intellectual property rights under the Agreement on Trade-Related Intellectual Property Rights (TRIPS). Others are permanent, for example, Article XVIII, Governmental Assistance to Economic Development, of the GATT.[4] A good case exists for both types of SDT in principle, but the specific instruments used arguably are often neither efficient nor effective.

In the run-up to the launch of the Doha round, developing countries pushed hard for an expansion and strengthening of SDT. The central issue confronting members is how to recast SDT in a way that would assist the development of low-income countries, be seen to do so by developing countries, and be regarded as both 'legitimate' and appropriate by developed country members. There is widespread agreement that as it stands today

SDT does not simultaneously ensure that developing countries see the WTO as a helpful institution and allow the membership as a whole to improve market access and multilateral rules through recurring rounds of negotiation. The discussions to date have not focused on the economics of SDT rules, that is, on the costs and benefits of alternative options. Instead, developing country proposals have largely emphasized the need for binding commitments for financial and technical assistance; for more flexibility and policy space, and implicitly if not explicitly the need to be able to restrict trade to promote development. Developed countries have rejected suggestions along these lines.

Since its first implementation, SDT has been hotly debated by trade-policy makers, academics and non-governmental organizations (NGOs). Discussions concentrated on the scope and size of the SDT measures, their effectiveness and side effects and who should be eligible and on what terms, the *i.e.* issue of graduation out of SDT. This is not the place to review the vast literature on this subject. Briefly stated the conclusions are that non-reciprocal trade preferences provide relatively small benefits for most recipient countries. Some tariff revenues are diverted to the exporter in the beneficiary country, but in ways that may subvert long-run development. They divert resources away from critical sectors, create inefficiencies, encourage rent-seeking rather than productive investment and may undermine incentives for trade liberalization. Indeed, a good case can be made that the approach is fundamentally flawed in that it helped create incentives for developing countries not to engage in the process of reciprocal liberalization of trade barriers and the rule-making process. It has also not helped the institution move forward in the rule-making arena. There is a need to recast SDT if the WTO is to become more effective in helping developing countries to use trade for development. There are two key dimensions: market access and WTO rules. On the former we argue in favour of less discrimination between WTO members. On the latter, conversely, we argue for more differentiation across developing countries: one size does not fit all.

Market access

Improved market access for developing countries' exports in goods and services through a lowering of trade barriers on a most-favoured nation (MFN) basis will have the largest beneficial impact on development. In particular, the high barriers on products that count for a large share of developing countries' exports, such as agriculture and labour-intensively produced products, should be lowered substantially. An appropriate formula approach to bring this about, with final dates and maximum tariff levels to be agreed upon, would do much to improve the relevance of the WTO from a development perspective. Developing countries should participate in the process by offering reciprocity, in terms of binding their tariffs and lowering the level of these tariffs. It is true that developed countries can and should stimulate exports from developing countries by further liberalization, but it should be noted as well that their trade barriers on an average are already low. Given that developing countries have higher barriers to trade, there is much scope to stimulate trade between developing countries by lowering barriers to trade in non-agricultural products. The potential for trade expansion between developing countries is particularly large given the relatively high growth rates of many middle-income countries. Moreover, as developing countries on an average have bound a lower share of their tariffs, and current ceiling bindings are often much higher than applied tariff rates, much can be done by low-income countries to participate in the WTO process without necessarily having a large impact on applied levels of protection.

More access to services markets, especially with respect to Mode 4 services, could have a significant impact on development prospects, as could further expansion of commitments by developing countries on inward FDI in services (Mode 3). Research summarized in Hoekman *et al.* (2004) suggests that the potential gains from services liberalization, especially Mode 4 access to markets of developed countries, as well as continued liberal policy stances towards Mode 1 transactions (cross-border trade), may have a more significant beneficial impact than merchandise trade reforms may have. This agenda should therefore be given more attention than has been the case to date.

These proposals can do much to help achieve both the income target of the Millennium Development Goals (MDGs) as well as other goals. In our view market access should be pursued primarily on an MFN basis, span both goods and services and rely on the mechanics of reciprocity. This is not a new suggestion – this type of SDT dates back to the 1960s (Hudec 1987) – with the differential treatment comprising an acceptance on the part of the major WTO members (large markets) to eliminate tariffs and other trade barriers on the goods, and now also services, in which developing countries have a comparative advantage. Deep preferences should be reserved for the least-developed countries (LDCs). Improvement by full coverage of products and simplification of rules of origin should increase the effectiveness of these preferences. MFN-based trade liberalization does not imply the immediate end of current preference programmes – countries are unlikely to move to free trade. Improving the functioning of existing preference programmes would provide some additional value to the countries that benefit from preferences during the period in which MFN rates are reduced.

However, preferences are not a long-term solution, as noted earlier, they come at a high cost to excluded countries, and may not benefit recipients much either.[5] In order to assist low-income countries to benefit from market access opportunities, a significant increase is needed in technical and financial assistance to support programmes to facilitate adjustment, expand supply capacity and improve the investment climate. The need for this is acute in absolute terms, but is made even stronger as the trading system moves in the direction of lower MFN trade barriers and the consequent erosion of preferences for those countries that currently benefit from effective preferential access. What is required is a de-linking of development assistance from trade policy – a shift from the current strategy of permitting a small subset of countries to benefit from the large distortions created by developed countries on their markets, to a policy that puts the emphasis on direct support to expand trade capacity and improve performance.

WTO rules

A distinction can be made between core rules and other rules. The core rules span MFN, national treatment, binding tariffs and the ban on quantitative restrictions. These rules should apply to all members. Currently they do not, in part because of specific provisions in the GATT, for example, Article XVIII, Governmental Assistance to Economic Development, and in part because of the Enabling Clause which, for example, provides much more leeway for developing countries to discriminate in favour of each other in the context of regional integration, and allows for limited reciprocity in terms of tariff bindings. We do not deny that weak institutional capacity and severe market imperfections combined with lack of financial resources may require that developing countries pursue second-best trade policies. However, existing WTO provisions – safeguards, waivers and renegotiation – already provide ample scope for countries to do so. In moving towards a uniform approach for the core rules, provision could be made for one-off, time-limited exceptions (Keck and Low 2003), but in principle these should have universal applicability. Note that an implication of this suggestion is that some basic WTO provisions should be reconsidered.

A different approach is proposed for the other WTO rules. The reciprocal exchange of trade liberalization commitments benefits all countries that engage in the process – one reason why we believe the core WTO trade-policy rules should apply to all members. The value of reciprocity when applied to regulatory policies are much more doubtful, given analysts' uncertainty about the appropriateness of particular policy instruments, and the differences between countries' domestic priorities (Hoekman 2002). A good case can be made that when it comes to regulatory policies that affect trade only indirectly if at all, one quickly gets into a situation where apples are traded for oranges, with significant potential for a negative net outcome for low-income countries. This suggests that attention should focus on redefining the principle of calibrated reciprocity in the Enabling Clause to apply only to policy disciplines that are resource-intensive to implement or that may not be development priorities for poor-and-small developing economies. An example is the TRIPS agreement. This will require more differentiation between developing countries. When it comes to future rule making, to some extent this can be achieved through the choice of negotiating modalities, such as a GATS-type positive-list approach. However, this may not always be feasible, and will be difficult to apply to existing disciplines.[6]

Our views in this regard are simple: low-income and small economies should receive SDT for resource-intensive agreements; others should not. Although this has been a politically sensitive issue in the WTO, much of the discussion on more country differentiation has implicitly, if not explicitly, been driven by market access preferences, where country classification is inherently arbitrary. In the case of implementation of resource-intensive WTO agreements, a more general approach based on objective criteria could resolve many of the issues. As discussed in Hoekman *et al.* (2004), this would entail the right for a specific group of low-income and small economies – to be negotiated – to opt out of such agreements. To allow for flexibility, the criteria adopted for differentiation could be supplemented by a fairly demanding appeals procedure for countries that feel they have been particularly hurt as a result of not satisfying the criteria.

SDT negotiations since Doha

During 2002–03, the SDT debate in the WTO focused on 88 specific proposals made by developing countries relating to existing agreements and provisions, with some discussion of a possible new 'Framework Agreement' and a Monitoring Mechanism to track delivery of SDT and its effectiveness. The various proposals can be classified into four categories: (1) calls for improved preferential access to industrialized country markets; (2) exemptions from specific WTO rules[7]; (3) binding and enforceable promises to provide technical and financial assistance to help developing countries implement multilateral rules; (4) expansion of development aid to address supply constraints that restrict the ability of firms to take advantage of improved market access.

The discussion on SDT was plagued by procedural and substantive disagreements. In an effort to break the impasse, the Chair of the General Council offered in the spring of 2003 a procedure for dealing with the proposals that had been tabled. The WTO Ministerial of Cancun did not bring progress in the SDT negotiations. Almost one year later, the WTO General Council agreed upon a framework for modalities to continue the Doha Round (WT/L/579). This Doha Work Programme (DWP) instructs the WTO bodies that negotiate on SDT 'to expeditiously continue their work' and to come up with clear recommendations for decisions in July 2005 at the latest.

Proposals related to technical assistance and information/transparency have been accepted. Some other proposals spanned suggestions relating to rules on regional integration, anti-dumping, subsidies, agriculture, GATS, dispute settlement, sanitary and phytosanitary standards (SPS), TRIMS, safeguards and TRIPS. Several of these proposals, for example, on TRIPS and Agriculture, make good sense.[8] However, we disagree with others, for example, on some of the proposals to reduce restraints in the use of trade measures to address balance-of-payments difficulties as these are deemed to be incompatible with good development practice. As mentioned, disciplines in this area should in our view be part of the core rules of the WTO and apply for all members. We also feel that some other proposals, for example, the proposal to exempt LDCs from the TRIMS agreement, or the suggestion that LDCs, 'notwithstanding any provision of any WTO Agreement, shall not be required to implement or comply with obligations that are prejudicial to their individual development needs…'[9] are too open-ended to be beneficial.

What the current approach to SDT, including efforts to narrow the gaps in Cancun,[10] does not do is go beyond the Doha Ministerial mandate. While this is understandable, in our view it is inadequate. There is now an opportunity to rethink the framework for SDT in the WTO. This is as much a forward-looking issue as it is a backward-looking issue, dealing with existing rules. Both types of issues are best addressed in the context of a new framework agreement for SDT, one that takes a cross-cutting approach. The DWP explicitly demands that the Committee on Trade and Development address the cross-cutting issues and the incorporation of SDT treatment into the architecture of WTO rules.[11] The need for a rethinking arguably increased post-Cancun. If a good framework for SDT had been in place that ensured that poor and/or small countries would not be subject to significant downside risks from accepting to negotiate on the Singapore Issues, the Cancun meeting might have ended successfully.

What might a new framework encompass? Abstracting from the important question of country differentiation, elements of a possible new approach could include:[12]

i   Acceptance of the core rules by all WTO members: MFN, national treatment, the ban on quotas, binding of maximum tariffs and commitments to gradually lower these bindings and open service markets to greater competition in negotiating rounds.

ii   More reliance on explicit cost–benefit analysis to identify net implementation benefits for countries and whether existing instruments impose negative (pecuniary) spillovers on other countries.

iii For a set of agreed resource-intensive and 'non-core' rules, adoption of a mechanism that generates information on objectives and effectiveness of applied policies that are (alleged to be) inconsistent with WTO disciplines, as well as information on the extent of any negative spillovers and the need for financial and technical assistance. Moving away from opt outs and arbitrary transition periods and towards a process that involves policy dialogue and accountability could do much to enhance the development relevance of the WTO, while at the same time reducing the perceived downside risk of undertaking new commitments.

iv   Shifting towards more efficient transfer/assistance mechanisms as part of a transition away from trade preferences, with aid directed at priority areas defined in national development plans and strategies, with clear accountability on the delivery of assistance.

Acknowledgement

This chapter is based on Hoekman *et al.* (2004). We are grateful to Gerrit Faber for assistance in preparing this chapter.

Notes

1 See Hart and Dymond (2003), Keck and Low (2003), Michalopoulos (2001), Oyejide (2002), Stevens (2002), Page (2001), Pangestu (2000), Whalley (1999) and Youssef (1999) for complementary analyses.

2 The *ex post* dimension to the asymmetric balance of rulemaking in the WTO has arguably been most important historically, in that rules that are perceived to be 'too difficult' to abide by are only honoured in the breach – for example, the GATT Article XI ban on quantitative restrictions and disciplines on trade-distorting policies in agriculture, for which the US obtained a waiver in 1955. See Hoekman and Kostecki (2001) and Michalopoulos (2001) for further discussion and references to the literature.

3 For a succinct but comprehensive summary of the post-Doha SDT discussions in the WTO, see the ICTSD/IISD Doha Round Briefing Series, Vol. 1, No. 13, February 2003 (www.ictsd.org).

4 GATT Article XVIII allows developing countries to use trade policies in the pursuit of industrial development objectives and to protect the balance of payments, imposing weaker disciplines than on industrialized countries. There are also many exhortations to developed countries to 'take into account' the interests of the developing countries in the application of WTO rules and disciplines.

5 They are also very inefficient transfer mechanisms. The costs to the EU and USA of providing 1 US dollar of preferential access has been estimated to exceed 5 US dollars (The World Bank 2003).

6 In the case of the Singapore Issues, for example, a positive-list approach can be applied to trade facilitation. But such an approach will be more difficult to apply to issues such as procurement or competition policy if multilateral disciplines are to have meaning.

7 These imply either more freedom to use restrictive trade policies that are otherwise subject to WTO disciplines, or exemptions from rules requiring the adoption of common regulatory or administrative disciplines.

8 Some proposals have already been agreed in other fora, for example, the recent TRIPS Council decision for a review mechanism of developed country efforts to provide incentives for technology transfer to LDCs under Article 66.2 of TRIPS. Hoekman, *et al.* (2004) discuss policy options to encourage technology transfer in more depth.

9 Proposal by the African Group, TN/CTD/W/3/Rev. 2.

10 In Cancun, a number of additional proposals were accepted by members on an *ad referendum* basis.

11 The DWP refers to a report of the Committee on Trade and Development (TN/CTD/7) that lists the following cross-cutting issues: principles and objectives of SDT, single or multi-tiered structure of rights and obligations, coherence, benchmarking, technical assistance and capacity building, transition periods, trade preferences including the Enabling Clause, utilization and universal or differentiated treatment including graduation.

12 What follows draws on Hoekman (2004).

References

Bhagwati, J. (1988) *Protectionism*, Cambridge, MA: MIT Press.

Finger, J.M. (1991) 'Development economics and the GATT', in J. De Melo and A. Sapir (eds) *Trade Theory and Economic Reform*, Cambridge, MA: Basil Blackwell.

Hart, M. and Dymond, B. (2003) 'Special and differential treatment and the Doha "Development" Round', *Journal of World Trade*, 37: 395–415.

Hoekman, B. (2002) 'Strengthening the global trade architecture for development: The post-Doha agenda', *World Trade Review*, 1: 23–46.

Hoekman, B. (2004) 'Operationalizing the concept of policy space in the WTO: beyond Special and Differential Treatment', mimeo, Washington, DC: The World Bank.

Hoekman, B. and Kostecki, M. (2001) *The Political Economy of the World Trading System*, Oxford: Oxford University Press.

Hoekman, B., Maskus, K. and Saggi, K. (2004) 'Transfer of technology to developing countries: unilateral and multilateral policy options', Policy Research Working Paper 3332, Washington, DC: The World Bank.

Hoekman, B., Michalopoulos, C. and Winters, L.A. (2004) 'Special and differential treatment of developing countries in the WTO: moving forward after Cancun', *The World Economy*, 27: 481–506.

Hudec, R. (1987) *Developing Countries in the GATT Legal System*, London: Trade Policy Research Centre.

Irwin, D. (2001) *Free Trade Under Fire*, Princeton, NJ: Princeton University Press.

Keck, A. and Low, P. (2003) 'Special and differential treatment in the WTO: why, when and how?', mimeo, Geneva: WTO.

Michalopoulos, C. (2000) 'The role of Special and Differential Treatment for developing countries in GATT and the WTO', Policy Research Working Paper No. 2388, Washington, DC: The World Bank.

Michalopoulos, C. (2001) *Developing Countries in the WTO*, New York: Palgrave.

Oyejide, T.A. (2002) 'Special and differential treatment', in B. Hoekman, P. English and A. Matto (eds) *Development, Trade and the WTO: A Handbook*, Washington, DC: The World Bank.

Page, S. (2001) 'Country classifications and trade', report for DFID, mimeo, London: Overseas Development Institute.

Pangestu, M. (2000) 'Special and differential treatment: special for whom and how different?', *The World Economy*, 23: 1285–1302.

Stevens, C. (2002) 'The future of SDT for developing countries in the WTO', mimeo, Sussex: Institute for Development Studies.

Whalley, J. (1999) 'Special and differential treatment in the Millennium Round', *The World Economy*, 22: 1065–1093.

World Bank, The (2003) *Global Economic Prospects and the Developed Countries*, Washington, DC: The World Bank.

Youssef, H. (1999) 'Special and differential treatment for developing countries in the WTO', Working Paper No. 2, Geneva: South Centre.

7 The role of the G-20

Jolanda E. Ygosse Battisti, Julia von Maltzan Pacheco and Fabiana D'Atri

Introduction

Late August 2003, in the run-up to the World Trade Organization (WTO) Ministerial of Cancun, a coalition of 20 developing countries, referred to as G-20, was formed. The members of this heterogeneous group shared the position that they considered the Joint EC–US Paper on Agriculture, released on 13 August (WTO 2003a), inadequate and falling short of the ambitions laid down in the Doha Development Agenda (DDA). This group of developing countries, 11 of which are among the members of the Cairns Group, presented a common view in a joint framework proposal (G-20 2003) addressing the three pillars of agricultural negotiations: market access, export competition and domestic support.

This chapter studies the potential role of this large and diverse coalition in negotiations on the DDA by taking a game-theoretic model of international trade policy negotiations, in which the G-20 forms what we label a 'commitment coalition'. Sceptics have argued that such a coalition is not stable, and that opposing proposals made by the developed countries may do more harm than good to the economies of the G-20. It is true that membership of the coalition has changed in the course of time. At the time that Brazil took the initiative to form a coalition for the upcoming trade negotiations in Cancun, it started out with a modest group of five countries. The common proposal on agriculture of 20 August 2003 reflected the views of 20 members but during subsequent negotiations, a number of Latin American countries with tight links to the USA dropped out of the coalition, giving rise to predictions of a collapse of the newly formed group. However, new countries substituted the dropouts, and attempts to break down this new player in the international negotiating arena thus far have not been successful. Colombia, Costa Rica, Ecuador, El Salvador and Peru are co-sponsors of the Agriculture Framework Proposal (WTO 2003b). They left the coalition as a result of bilateral trade agreements with the USA. Egypt,

Indonesia, Nigeria, Tanzania and Zimbabwe have joined the coalition at a later stage. Currently the G-20 includes five African countries (Egypt, Nigeria, South Africa, Tanzania and Zimbabwe), six Asian countries (China, India, Indonesia, Pakistan, The Philippines and Thailand) and ten Latin American countries (Argentina, Bolivia, Brazil, Chile, Cuba, Guatemala, Mexico, Paraguay, Uruguay and Venezuela).

The literature on international policy conflict and the impact of coalitions shows that if a credible commitment technology or trigger mechanism exists, the coalition can be stable and beneficiary to its members. We argue that there exists such a natural commitment mechanism that ensures the robustness of the coalition and a positive outcome for the G-20 countries. Moreover, by extending the three-country model to an n-country model, we show that due to entry of new members into the G-20 the potential of developed countries to break the coalition is limited. One of the main conclusions is that the G-20 play an important role in enforcing a genuine commitment of the developed countries to act according to the Doha Mandate.

The G-20

While geographically diverse, the members of the G-20 have in common that agriculture generates a substantial share of overall income and employment in their economies, and that agricultural development may contribute critically to poverty alleviation. On an average, 50.7 per cent of their working population is engaged in the agricultural sector. This sector represents around 20 per cent of Gross Domestic Product (GDP), compared to only 2 per cent in the USA (The World Bank 2005, Table 1). Overall, 70 per cent of the world agricultural population lives in the G-20 countries, compared to less than 1 per cent in the USA and EU-15, put together.

As the scenario studies by Anderson *et al.* in Chapter 2 of this volume show, agricultural producers' welfare could improve significantly by trade liberalization. This holds even though not all G-20 members are net exporters of agricultural products. Before embarking on the game-theoretic analysis, some key statistics will be presented pertaining to the widely different trade positions of the main players in world trade in agricultural products.

Figure 7.1 shows the changing positions of the USA, EU and the G-20 during the period 1980–2003. The substantial net positive trade balance for agricultural products of the USA during the second half of the 1980s and the 1990 has turned into a negative trade balance position in the early years of the new millennium. In the case of the EU, the negative trade balance has tended to decrease both in absolute and relative terms since the late 1980s. It should be noted that EU data include intra-EU trade and consequently do not represent the net trade positions towards the rest of the world. Not unlikely, the EU

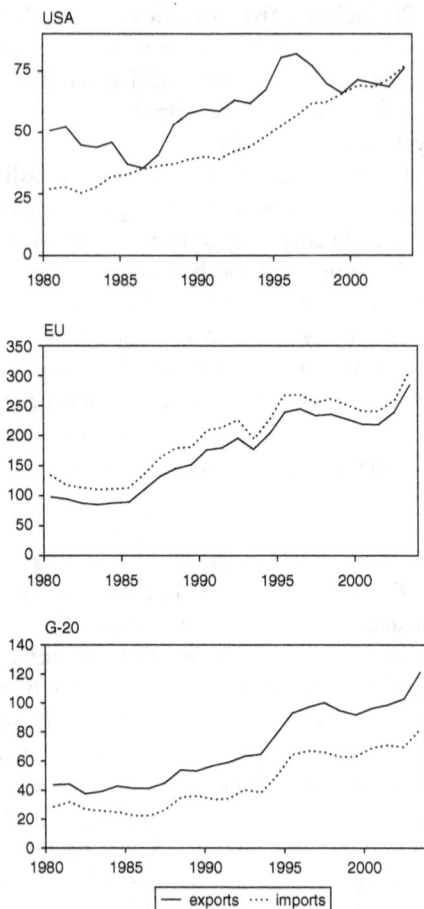

Figure 7.1 Agricultural exports and imports of the USA, the EU and the G-20, in billions of US dollars, 1980–2003.

Source: WTO statistics (http://www.wto.org/english/res_e/statis_e/statis_e.htm).

position will change substantially in the years ahead, due to the accession of ten new member states in May 2004. The aggregate position of the G-20 countries shows a widening net positive trade balance. However, there is substantial within group variation in net trade positions, as shown in Figure 7.2. Argentina, Brazil, Chile, India, Indonesia, South Africa and Thailand are among the countries showing positive trade balances throughout most of the period. China, Egypt, Mexico, Nigeria, Pakistan, the Philippines and Venezuela show negative trade balances throughout nearly all of the period under investigation. This variation illustrates that members of the G-20 not only share common interests in their negotiations with the EU and USA, but also may represent different interests regarding market access, export subsidies, domestic support and Special and Differential Treatment (SDT).

G-20 proposals

In setting the trade rules for the last five decades, it has been in the interests of the USA and the EU to exclude the agricultural sector from the liberalization process, at least up to the Uruguay Round, thus creating a conflict of interests with G-20 and other developing countries that are in favour of improved market access. As such, this historical position gives little credibility to the USA and the EU as leaders in agricultural liberalization talks – key to the DDA. The lack of credibility may in part be fuelled as well by the largely unresolved issue of implementation of the rules agreed in the Uruguay Round.

The G-20 proposal for the Cancun Ministerial, as laid down in document WT/MIN(03)/W/6, only addresses the agricultural framework, thereby clearly signalling that progress in the area of agricultural trade is required to make progress in other areas of the agenda. The G-20 text proposes much stronger cuts in domestic support of agriculture in developed countries than proposed in the Joint EC-US Paper on Agriculture. For example, while the joint EC–US proposal suggests some minor changes in Article 6.5 of the Agreement on Agriculture (AoA), Domestic Support Commitments, the G-20 calls for the elimination of this article, which allows direct payments under production-limiting programmes outside the commitments to reduce domestic support.

On market access, the G-20 proposal is much more specific than the joint EC-US proposal, demanding 'market access for all products, in an effective and measurable way'. Moreover, it asks for strict rules on administration of tariff rate quotas (TRQ): that TRQs should be expanded to a percentage of domestic absorption, and that in-quota tariff rates should be reduced to zero. Moreover, developing countries should not be required to make commitments on TRQ expansion and in-quota tariff rate reduction.

Another important difference between the EC–US and the G-20 proposals is the call for abolishment of the Special Safeguards (SSGs) in the AoA for developed countries. SSGs are very hard to control, and easily abused to keep 'unwanted' imports out. Access of tropical products and other agricultural products from developing countries to markets of developed countries is explicitly demanded. On the elimination of export subsidies the G-20 proposal sets a much clearer timetable.

Overall, the proposal shows that the G-20 intends to keep developed countries to their commitment in the Doha Declarations. This becomes even

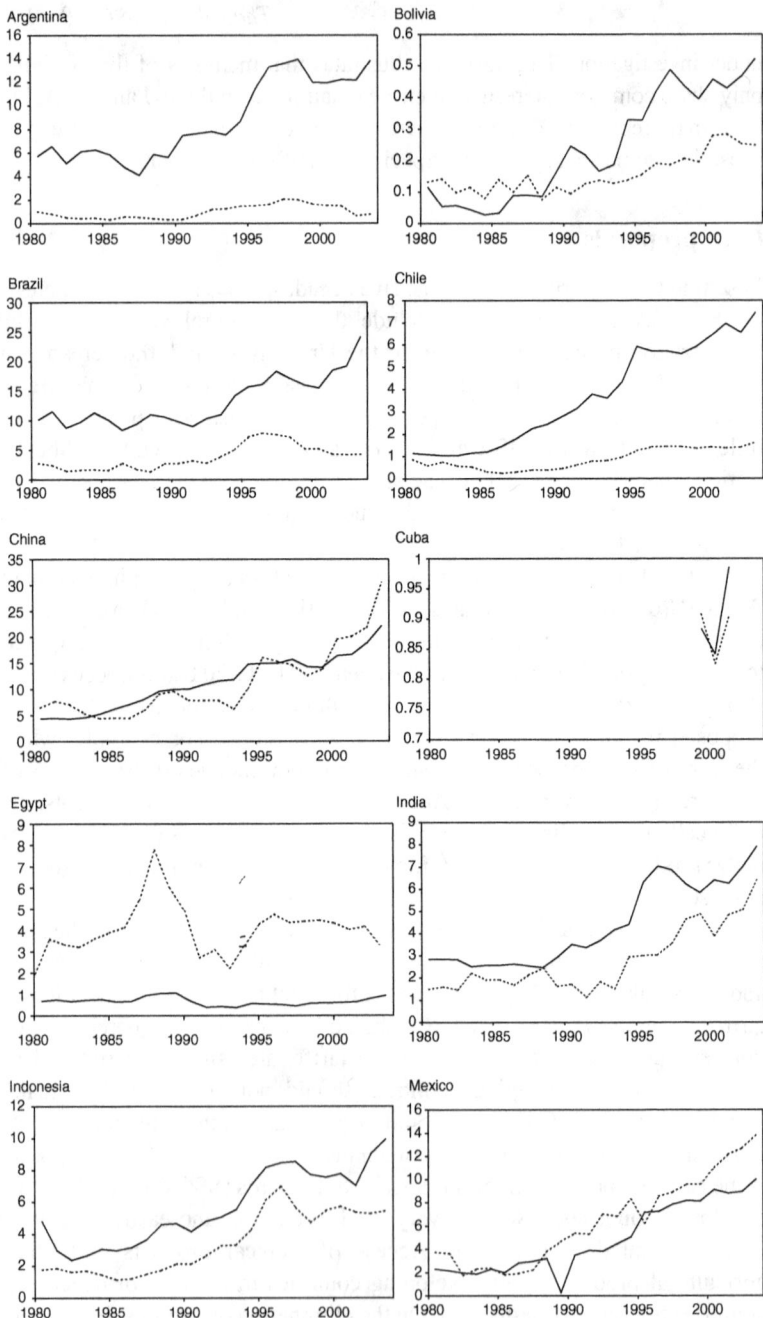

Figure 7.2 Agricultural exports and imports of the G-20 countries, in millions of US dollars, 1980–2003.

Source: WTO statistics (http://www.wto.org/english/res_e/statis_e/statis_e.htm).

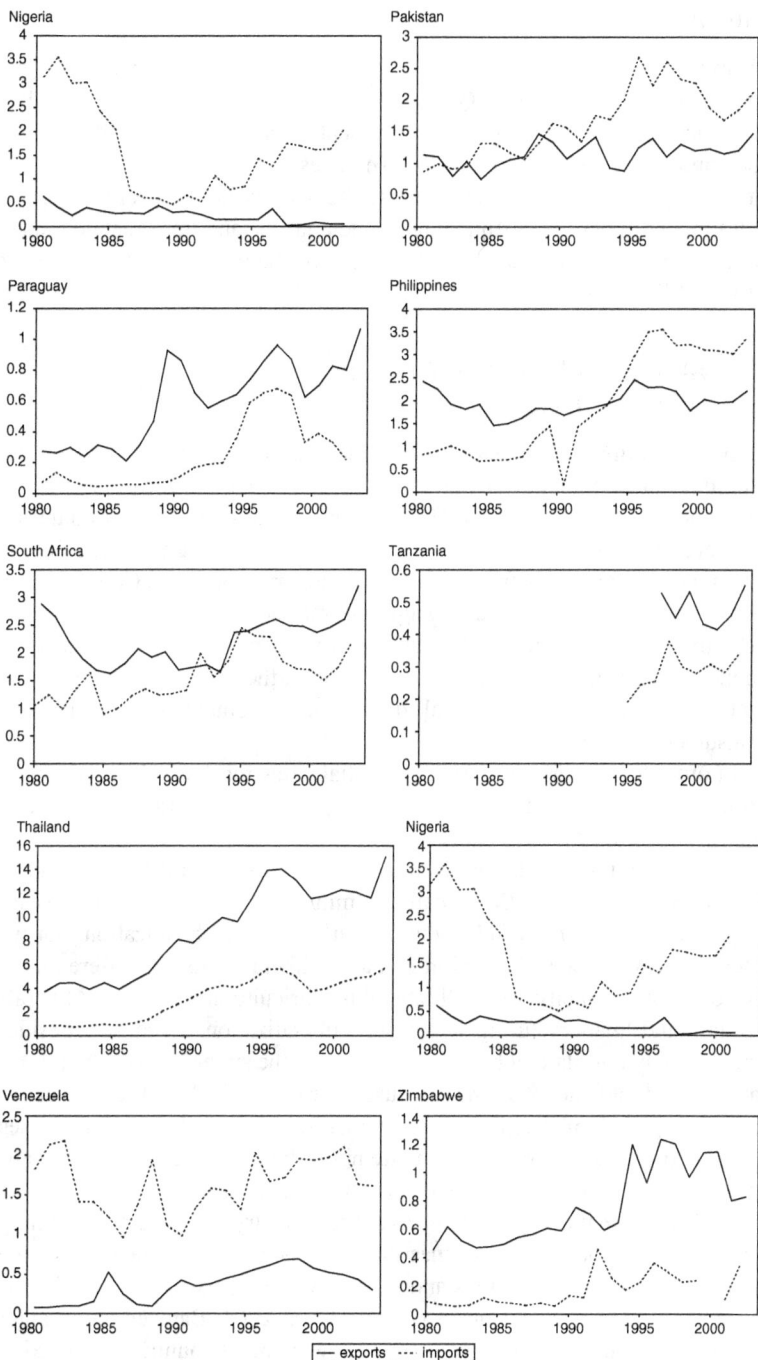

Figure 7.2 Continued.

clearer in a more recently issued proposal on May 28, 2004, specifically on market access (G-20 2004). Quoting the Doha Ministerial Declaration that countries agreed to 'substantial improvement in market access', and recalling the commitment to SDT, the G-20 formulates a set of measures that would effectively achieve the Doha Mandate. This proposal also calls for clear rules on cutting tariffs, abandoning in-quota tariffs, and immediate elimination of SSGs, and formulates clearly what steps should be taken to effectively provide SDT.

The advantage of coalition-forming: new talks, new rules

General equilibrium simulations, as presented in Chapter 2 of this volume by Anderson *et al.*, show that all regions stand to gain most from full liberalization of agricultural trade. The outcomes of these models for countries that heavily protect their agricultural sector are to a large extent due to consumer welfare gains from lifting distortionary protection. Conservatism of the USA and the EU regarding agricultural trade liberalization can therefore only be explained by a political-economy argument: they attribute higher weights in their welfare function to what their agricultural producers stand to lose from agricultural liberalization compared to what their consumers stand to gain.

In order to gain insight into the potential gains for the G-20 countries in forming a coalition in the WTO negotiation process, we take a game-theoretic approach. We follow closely the bargaining game described in Aghion *et al.* (2004). Our game is different in four aspects. First, we introduce an additional coalition concept, the so-called commitment coalition. Second, we do not restrict ourselves to full liberalization versus no liberalization, but we include in our model the option of partial liberalization in differentiated sectors. For simplicity, we shall label this 'agricultural sector only' liberalization, and 'manufacturing sector only' liberalization. Third, we consider initially only multilateral bargaining, as this is the suitable specification for multilateral trade negotiations, because the rules of the WTO require unanimous approval of multilateral agreements. Sequential bargaining does enter into the game though, as an attempt to break the commitment coalition. Fourth, we alternate the agenda-setter in the game.

We formulate initially the game as a three-country multilateral bargaining game. In fact, the model assumes that the leader country internalizes the welfare gains of the coalitions and is able to pass on part of this welfare as a transfer to the other countries (Aghion *et al.* 2004; Bagwell and Staiger 2004). Subsequently, we generalize by allowing more countries, mimicking the effect of countries leaving and entering the G-20, in a modified game that allows sequential bargaining by a high-income non-G-20 country as a mechanism to regain leadership.

The set up of the model is as follows. Three countries, a, b and c, can form commitment coalitions and free-trade coalitions. A commitment coalition can be interpreted as an informal agreement among a subset of countries, such as the G-20, to adopt a common negotiation position. This commitment coalition is credible if a commitment-enforcement mechanism exists, or if the costs of attempts to break the commitment coalition by a third country are too high. The second coalition form is defined similar to the definition used by Aghion *et al.* (2004) with the only difference that the free-trade coalition members can trade at zero tariffs within the coalition area only in the sector included in the coalition agreement. A free-trade coalition can include all sectors (T), the agricultural sector only (A) or the manufactured sector only (M). For simplicity, every country belongs to exactly one commitment coalition and one free-trade coalition. The structure of each type of coalition is defined as a partition Γ for a free-trade coalition and a partition Φ for a commitment coalition of the set $\{a,b,c\}$.

The commitment coalition structure is simple: all countries form a coalition, or only a and b, or only b and c form a coalition. The first can be interpreted as all WTO countries strongly and credibly committed to the Doha Mandate of development through trade, and therefore all in favour of a free-trade coalition including all sectors. With such a commitment coalition structure the game ends obviously in global free-trade including all sectors. The second structure can be interpreted as the G-20 coalition in favour of a free-trade coalition including all sectors, and a third party, conservative in liberalization of its agricultural sector. The third option becomes important when we consider possible strategies of country c to regain leadership.

We play the game first without a commitment coalition. In that case, the commitment coalition structure is defined as $\Phi = \langle\{a\},\{b\},\{c\}\rangle$. Without the commitment coalition, country c is the agenda-setter, and thus the leader in the game. We shall see that the leader optimizes his pay-off. Put differently, the leader gets what he wants. Next we play the game with the commitment coalition structure $\Phi = \langle\{ab\},\{c\}\rangle$. This new structure arises due to the announcement of the commitment coalition of their negotiation position. It alters the game in that it makes the commitment coalition the agenda-setter. The announcement can be interpreted as a simplified version of the G-20 proposal, in which the coalition only accepts further liberalization in other sectors, if full liberalization of the agricultural sector is dealt with first, or simultaneously. This could be seen as a strategic move, in which the commitment coalition limits its options in a way that yields a strategic advantage.

The pay-off to each country is assigned by a value function and depends on both the commitment as well as the free-trade coalition structures. We allow for differences in welfare gains for each country from trade liberalization in all sectors (T), the agricultural sector only (A) or the manufactured sector only (M). Here we shall not attempt to build the value functions from specific objective functions of each country with respect to the impact of trade agreements on national welfare. Instead, assumptions with respect to the different weights that countries give to gains and losses for consumers and producers in each sector are implicit in the pay-off structure.

The pay-offs are defined as follows. Let $W_T(abc)$ denote the joint pay-offs of the three countries under free trade in all sectors (T). Similarly, define $W_A(abc)$ as the joint pay-offs if only a free-trade agreement in the agricultural sector is reached and $W_M(abc)$ the joint pay-offs of a free-trade agreement in the sector of manufactures only. Considering all countries as two-sector economies, we have: $W_T(abc) = W_A(abc) + W_M(abc)$.

Let $W_{T,j}(abc)$ for all $j = a,b,c$ denote the pay-off of the j-th country under a complete free-trade agreement among all countries. $W_{A,j}(abc)$ and $W_{M,j}(abc)$ are defined in a similar way. For now we limit ourselves to multilateral bargaining only, and therefore there is no need to define the pay-offs of each country in case a free-trade sub-coalition is formed, nor to define the possible externalities to the country not included in such sub-coalition. Finally, let $W(j)$ denote country j's pay-off when there are no free-trade negotiations for all $j=a,b,c$.

In our game, countries a and b represent developing countries that are assumed to have everything to gain from universal free trade in all sectors. Country c represents developed countries, reluctant to liberalize their agricultural sector due to the relatively high weight they attach to the losses for home producers. We can formulate this in terms of pay-offs as follows:

$$W_{T,z}(abc) > W_{A,z}(abc) > W_{M,z}(abc) \text{ for all } z = a,b$$
$$W_{M,c}(abc) > W_{T,c}(abc) > W_{A,c}(abc)$$

Note that for country c universal free trade in all sectors is only second-best. The game is played as follows.

Game 1 – no commitment coalition exists, and country c is the agenda-setter

Country c is the leader and therefore sets the agenda. This role comes naturally to developed countries as in most international negotiation frameworks including the WTO 'money rules'. Country c makes a take-it-or-leave-it offer to countries a and b. The offer is to fully liberalize trade in sector

M, while leaving discussions on trade liberalization in sector A to a later date. If a and b accept, we have a multilateral agreement and the joint pay-off is $W_M(abc)$. Country c has maximized its own pay-off. Countries a and b are better off compared to no trade agreement, but worse off compared to liberalization of sector A only and compared to full trade liberalization (T). If a and b accept, c has no incentive to enter into further negotiations of liberalization of sector A in a later stage. The game ends with liberalization in those sectors strategic to country c, and agricultural sector liberalization remains an unsolved question. See Figure 7.3 Game 1 for the game tree.

Game 2 – countries a and b form a commitment coalition

Knowing the incentive structure of country c, there is an alternative game that countries a and b can play. By announcing that they will not accept further liberalization of sector M before the liberalization of sector A is resolved, they become the agenda-setter, and thus the leader in the game. The commitment coalition makes a take-it-or-leave-it offer to country c to liberalize trade in all sectors (T). If their announcement is credible, the joint pay-off is $W_T(abc)$. Note that this outcome is the best possible outcome for world welfare and for countries a and b. However, for country c this outcome is better than no agreement, but worse than sector M only liberalization. See Figure 7.3 Game 2 for the game tree.

Game 3 – multilateral bargaining game with sequential bargaining strategy of country c

We mentioned that the outcome of Game 2 is only credible if the commitment coalition cannot be broken. To explore this point further, we define country a as the initiative-taker to forming the commitment coalition, and country b as the follower within the coalition $\{ab\}$. Country c could be successful in breaking the coalition by offering sequential bargaining, first to b, potentially causing negative externalities to country a which in turn may result in country a accepting c's offer and the game result returns to joint pay-off $W_M(abc)$.[1] Sceptics may argue that this is exactly what would happen, and therefore that opposing proposals made by the developed countries may do more harm than good to the economies of the G-20. Figure 7.3 Game 3 shows the game tree for this bargaining strategy.

After rejecting the offer by the commitment coalition, country c enters into sequential bargaining with country b. As discussed earlier, country b had initially joined the initiative of country a hoping for the joint proposal to pay off. However, the coalition formed by a and b is informal, and we

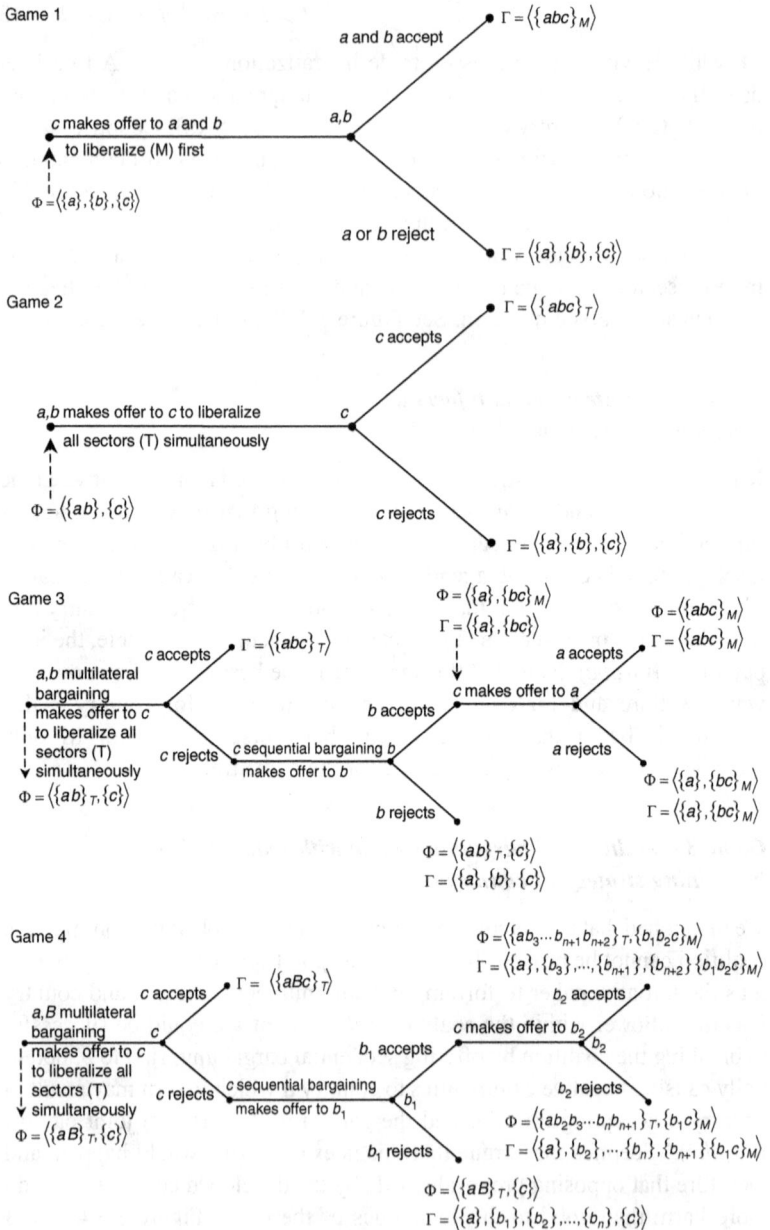

Game 1

c makes offer to a and b to liberalize (M) first

$\Phi = \langle \{a\}, \{b\}, \{c\} \rangle$

a,b

a and b accept — $\Gamma = \langle \{abc\}_M \rangle$

a or b reject — $\Gamma = \langle \{a\}, \{b\}, \{c\} \rangle$

Game 2

a,b makes offer to c to liberalize all sectors (T) simultaneously

$\Phi = \langle \{ab\}, \{c\} \rangle$

c

c accepts — $\Gamma = \langle \{abc\}_T \rangle$

c rejects — $\Gamma = \langle \{a\}, \{b\}, \{c\} \rangle$

Game 3

a,b multilateral bargaining makes offer to c to liberalize all sectors (T) simultaneously

$\Phi = \langle \{ab\}_T, \{c\} \rangle$

c accepts — $\Gamma = \langle \{abc\}_T \rangle$

c rejects — c sequential bargaining makes offer to b

b accepts

$\Phi = \langle \{a\}, \{bc\}_M \rangle$
$\Gamma = \langle \{a\}, \{bc\} \rangle$

c makes offer to a

a accepts — $\Phi = \langle \{abc\}_M \rangle$, $\Gamma = \langle \{abc\}_M \rangle$

a rejects — $\Phi = \langle \{a\}, \{bc\}_M \rangle$, $\Gamma = \langle \{a\}, \{bc\}_M \rangle$

b rejects — $\Phi = \langle \{ab\}_T, \{c\} \rangle$, $\Gamma = \langle \{a\}, \{b\}, \{c\} \rangle$

Game 4

a,B multilateral bargaining makes offer to c to liberalize all sectors (T) simultaneously

$\Phi = \langle \{aB\}_T, \{c\} \rangle$

c accepts — $\Gamma = \langle \{aBc\}_T \rangle$

c rejects — c sequential bargaining makes offer to b_1

b_1 accepts

$\Phi = \langle \{ab_3 \cdots b_{n+1}b_{n+2}\}_T, \{b_1b_2c\}_M \rangle$
$\Gamma = \langle \{a\}, \{b_3\}, \ldots, \{b_{n+1}\}, \{b_{n+2}\}\{b_1b_2c\}_M \rangle$

c makes offer to b_2

b_2 accepts

b_2 rejects — $\Phi = \langle \{ab_2b_3 \cdots b_nb_{n+1}\}_T, \{b_1c\}_M \rangle$, $\Gamma = \langle \{a\}, \{b_2\}, \ldots, \{b_n\}, \{b_{n+1}\}\{b_1c\}_M \rangle$

b_1 rejects — $\Phi = \langle \{aB\}_T, \{c\} \rangle$, $\Gamma = \langle \{a\}, \{b_1\}, \{b_2\}, \ldots, \{b_n\}, \{c\} \rangle$

Figure 7.3 Game trees of multilateral bargaining games with and without the G-20. (a) game 1 – Multilateral bargaining game – $\{c\}$ agenda setter (b) game 2 – Multilateral bargaining game – $\{ab\}$ agenda setter (c) game 3 – Mixed game: multilateral and sequential bargaining (d) game 4 – Mixed game: multilateral and sequential bargaining, allowing for replacement of 'drawn b' ($B = (b_1, b_2, b_3, \ldots, b_n)$).

have not discussed whether a commitment technology exists that assures stability of the coalition. Therefore, country b could consider leaving this coalition at no costs once it is clear that the commitment coalition proposal is rejected by country c. By accepting a bilateral deal with country c, country b can improve its welfare outcome as long as the pay-off country b gets when breaking the commitment coalition is larger than the pay-off country b gets if no trade agreement is made $W(b)$. The game ends like Game 1 because once country b has accepted a bilateral agreement, country a is better off to accept the offer country c makes in this sequential bargaining setting. This outcome seems to confirm the sceptics' critique that making agricultural trade liberalization a non-negotiable issue may do more harm than good to the economies of the G-20.

Game 4 – mixed game with *n* countries in commitment coalition

However, the result of Game 3 alters if we make the game more realistic, allowing for more countries in the commitment coalition with country a. We represent this as $B = (b_1, b_2, \ldots, b_n)$. Moreover, in case country c manages to take out one country, say b_1, of the commitment coalition, we allow for a new country to enter. For its next move, country c faces $B = (b_2, b_3, \ldots, b_{n+1})$. For any r countries with which country c manages to successfully negotiate bilaterally, r new countries will enter in the commitment coalition. The game tree is portrayed in Figure 7.3 Game 4 for bilateral negotiations by country c up to b_2. For country b_1 to accept c's offer, the pay-off to b_1 has to be higher than the future pay-off if b_1 sticks with the proposal of country a to demand agricultural sector liberalization first on the agenda. This gives the possibility that only countries (b) producing agricultural goods that do not conflict with country c's agricultural producers will have an incentive to defect, because country c can offer them a full trade liberalization without costs to its home agricultural producers. Put differently, country c can realize $W_{M,c}(bc)$ while country b gains $W_{T,b}(bc)$.

For country c to gain from the sequential game strategy, the commitment coalition should contain only countries with non-conflicting agricultural production. It is therefore in the interest of country a to replace defecting countries b with newcomers with which country a has more in common. The commitment coalition gains strength. This implies that attempts to break up the commitment coalition do not pay off. For $B = (b_1 b_2)$, if $W_{M,c}(b_1 c) < W_{T,c}(ab_1 b_2 c)$, then country c will be better of by accepting the commitment coalition's initial offer of universal free trade in all sectors. This can be generalized to n countries. Therefore we can state that if defecting countries b are replaced by countries who share common interest in agricultural production with country *a*, the commitment coalition grows stronger and becomes more difficult to defeat.

With the new player in the field, the decades-long hegemony of the USA and the EU in multilateral trade negotiations has been challenged. By firmly demanding progress on agricultural trade liberalization, the G-20 countries have managed to affect the rules of the game, and to change the agenda. Although sceptics predicted that the coalition would be short-lived, we show that the dynamics of exit and entry of new, more similar countries, can actually make the coalition stronger. A crucial factor for the robustness of the coalition is the credibility of the commitment mechanism of the G-20 countries.

Acknowledgement

We thank Marcelo Campos Battisti for his valuable comments on an earlier version of this text, and Cláudio Vieira and Guilherme Leite da Silva Dias for their contributions.

Note

1 Externalities can be positive, negative or zero. Here we abstract from the discussion on the impact of possible externalities. See Aghion *et al.* 2004.

References

Aghion, P., Antràs, P. and Helpman, E. (2004) 'Negotiating Free Trade', NBER Working Paper No. 10721.
Bagwell, K. and Staiger, R.W. (2004) 'Backward Stealing and Forward Manipulation in the WTO', NBER Working Paper No. 10420.
G-20 (2003) 'Agriculture Framework Proposal, Joint Proposal by Argentina, Brazil, Bolivia, China, Chile, Colombia, Costa Rica, Cuba, Ecuador, El Salvador, Guatemala, India, Mexico, Paraguay, Pakistan, Peru, Philippines, South Africa, Thailand, Venezuela', JOB(03)/162.
G-20 (2004) 'Proposal on a Framework for Establishing Modalities in Agriculture – Market Access', available online at http://www.g-20.gov.br (28 May 2004).
World Bank, The (2004) *World Development Report 2005: A Better Investment Climate For Everyone*, Washington, DC: The World Bank.
WTO (2003a) 'Joint EC-US Paper-Agriculture', JOB(03)/157, 13 August 2003.
WTO (2003b) WT/MIN(03)/W/6, 'Agricultural Framework Proposal', WTO Ministerial Conference, Fifth Session (formally documented proposal by G-20).

8 Minimum conditions for a package deal

An African perspective

Dominique Njinkeu and Nicola Loffler[1]

Introduction

Since the failure at Cancun, negotiations on the Doha Development Agenda (DDA) have focused on a number of divisive issues, including agriculture, cotton and the Singapore Issues. The environment during the build-up to the 2004 July General Council meeting was intense, as members were warned of the costs of failure of the July negotiations in terms of undermining multilateralism. Peter Sutherland, Chairman of the Director General's consultative board, warned 'that the institution [World Trade Organization (WTO)] and, indeed, multilateralism in international trade relations [would not] survive unharmed a failure to relaunch the Doha trade negotiations that foundered in Cancun last year' (Sutherland 2004). After marathon negotiations, agreement was reached on the Doha Work Programme (DWP) that provides a roadmap for the future phase of negotiations on modalities.

From an African perspective, the DWP contains both positive and negative elements. The positive elements include: the dropping of three of the four Singapore Issues, the commitment to end agricultural export subsidies, the inclusion of development provisions to address some African and other concerns of developing countries. On the negative side, there is a need for vigilance as many of the difficult issues have been left for the next phase of negotiations.

This chapter presents the main features of the DWP, viewed from an African perspective. It also considers African interests and concerns during the modalities phase of the negotiations. We shall highlight areas in which both positive and negative agendas will have to be pursued, with particular attention for the areas of agriculture and Special and Differential Treatment (SDT). Services, Non-Agricultural Market Access (NAMA) and trade facilitation will be discussed more briefly.

Agriculture

Agriculture has been the first priority for African negotiators since the launch of the DDA. Agriculture is particularly important to African countries as a source of employment and the generation of export revenues, as well as for reasons of food security and rural development. The performance of African agriculture has been reduced by the high levels of protection of agriculture in developed countries. African interests in the negotiations on agriculture have been twofold. First, their positive agenda has been to reduce the distortions in markets of developed countries, largely resulting from domestic support and export subsidies, as well as the trade-restrictive effects of standards and other non-tariff barriers (NTBs). Second, on the defensive side, African countries need flexibility to protect their local producers from competition from subsidized imports, through a variety of mechanisms including subsidies, tariffs and safeguards. In addition, certain African countries have an interest in protecting their preferential access to the markets of developed countries. Another shared concern relates to compliance with trade standards and to address supply-side constraints.

The DWP attempts at addressing many of these issues, with varying degrees of success, as will be examined later. In order to understand the outcome of the DWP negotiations, an appreciation of the political trade-offs involved in the agreement is necessary. As will be analysed later, the text offers a 'safe-haven' for some non-green domestic support payments through the expansion of the Blue Box; it also establishes the foundation for a wide exception in order to shield certain 'sensitive' products. In addition, the DWP prevents a re-assessment of Green Box rules and disciplines, allowing the possibility of continued support to farmers with subsidies, albeit delinked from production, but without any limits in volume. The problem with the DWP is that the provisions provide too much flexibility in these highly sensitive areas, which could have the effect of legitimizing the continuation of high levels of support, to the detriment of competing exporters, including many African countries. These compromises need to guide the pursuit of African interests and future strategies. They need to pay attention to the three pillars of the agriculture negotiations, and ensure horizontal integration of operationally effective SDT.

Domestic support

One of Africa's central interests in the negotiations on agriculture has been the reduction of trade-distorting domestic support (African Union 2004), which undermines the ability of African producers to compete in international markets (Watkins and von Braun 2003). It is important to note that subsidies may also have benefits, that is, by reducing prices for consumers of these products.

Of the 20 countries identified by Hoekman *et al.* (2002) as being significantly impacted by subsidies in developed countries, 12 are African. Under the Uruguay Round Agreement on Agriculture (AoA), the major problem with domestic support provisions resulted from 'the *de facto* reverse Special and Differential Treatment' granted to developed countries (Messerlin 2004). Such reversed special treatment was obtained primarily through calculations of the Aggregate Measure of Support (AMS) and selection of base levels, the lack of product-specific commitments and the insufficient level of discipline on trade-distorting support.

At face value, the DWP seems to advance the aim of 'substantial reductions' in trade-distorting support. In general, the tiered formula is positive, as it aims to harmonize levels of support. In addition, the 20 per cent downpayment in first year reductions is a welcome development although there is no guarantee of actual substantial reductions due to the water in the schedules of the EU and the USA, as shown in the following paragraphs.

Aggregate versus product-specific support

In the AoA, reduction commitments were based on aggregate levels, rather than being product-specific, which allowed for increases in expenditures on some products. The DWP makes minimal attempt at rectifying this problem, which is of crucial importance to African countries. As many African countries are dependent on one or two commodities, it is in their interest that subsidy cuts are made on a product of interest to them. When it became clear in the Cancun lead-up that no product-specific AMS reduction approach would be endorsed in the agricultural modalities, four West and Central African countries (Benin, Burkina Faso, Chad and Mali) tabled at the WTO General Council – that is, outside the framework of the general agriculture negotiations – a proposal on a Sectoral Initiative for Cotton. In this proposal, the four countries called for the total phasing out of all subsidies related to cotton production and trade. During the Doha negotiations, some developing country proposals demanded product-specific commitments. However, the DWP imposes no effective discipline. The text requires the capping of product-specific AMS, but no reduction commitments beyond those imposed for combined support. Although the text suggests that the AMS reductions 'will result in reductions of some product-specific support', this seems to be a statement of fact rather than a binding commitment. In fact, this is a step backwards from the binding language in the first draft that said: 'some of these product-specific caps will then be reduced' (WTO 2004a). This does perhaps open the door to a fast-track or early-harvest approach. However, the capping of AMS product-specific support will not be entirely effective as the AMS does not include Blue Box subsidies. Hence, the increase in some support is still imaginable by means of box shifting to the Blue Box. The potential for this box shifting could be limited if negotiations reinforce the language in paragraphs 7 and 8 pertaining to the overall reduction commitment for the aggregate of trade-distorting support, which includes AMS, Blue Box and *de minimis*.

African countries could secure reduction on products of interest to them through proposals for 'fast-track' or 'early harvest' reductions on certain commodities, or an innovative compensation scheme. The first option could involve the phasing in of product-specific support reductions based on development needs. This will be obtained by way of fast-track reductions for products that compete with developing country exports, starting with cotton and other commodities that are of crucial importance. There is some precedent for such a move based on the market access commitments for tropical products in the Uruguay Round.

In order to select products for a potential fast-track proposal, African countries would have to look both at the potential price increases in addition to the importance of these commodities for African exports. Research by The World Bank has highlighted the potential for price increases for many commodities of export interest to African countries, should liberalization successfully occur, with figures of 10–20 per cent for cotton, 20–40 per cent for dairy, 10–20 per cent for groundnuts, 33–90 per cent for rice and 20–40 per cent for sugar (Hoekman *et al.* 2002). Reductions would occur more quickly with 'a commitment by developed countries to the elimination of all production and export subsidies on commodities the consumption of which is primarily in the developed world' (Stiglitz and Charlton 2004) over the shortest possible period. This would ensure the effective implementation of the DWP goal of 'reductions of some product-specific support' (WTO 2004b: Para. 9).

Alternatively, further consideration should be given to the possibility of establishing a transitional compensatory scheme, which would ensure compensation for developing countries while support levels remain detrimental to their interests. This would, in effect be the opposite of a preference erosion compensation scheme, that is, compensation would be granted in situations where liberalization is not occurring, rather than compensation for the impact of liberalization when it does successfully occur, as in the case of preference erosion. Such a mechanism could be established along the lines of the Cotton Initiative with a comprehensive coverage of all commodities of interest to low-income countries. The amount of compensation would depend on the actual level of support to a specific product, and would decline as subsidies are reduced (Werth and Lee 2004). WTO members will need to give urgent attention to a number of practical issues associated with such a mechanism. This would compel the WTO to administer a transfer of funds between members. In addition, the relevant analytical tools to assess the impact of the subsidies on each country should be considered as a matter of priority. Similarly, the fast-track approach would be a significant departure from the aggregate rather than commodity-specific focus of the WTO AoA.

Base levels

Another problem in the AoA is the selection of base periods. The AMS base period 1986–88 is characterized by exceptionally high levels of protection (FAO 2003a). As a result of these severely inflated base levels, there is a significant leeway between permitted and existing levels of support. For example in 1999, the USA was providing subsidies at only 43 per cent of AMS (Hart and Beghin 2004). Clearly, this leeway reduces the effectiveness of AMS reduction commitments. Although there is little that can be done to address this problem in relation to the AMS, the issue is certainly relevant in relation to the base level that will be designated for the Blue Box.

Blue Box

The Blue Box exempts support for production-limiting schemes from reduction commitments. In the past, only six countries have used the Blue Box. The Blue Box programmes that the USA used were eliminated in 1996. It was originally intended that the Blue Box be eliminated at the end of the DDA. As a result, the Blue Box was considered a 'non-issue' during the negotiations before and at Cancun, attracting minimal attention from developing country negotiators. However, contrary to the predicted elimination, the DWP actually expands Blue Box coverage to direct payments decoupled from production but not from prices (WTO 2004b: Para. 13.2). This is likely to protect the counter-cyclical payments established by the USA under the US 2002 Farm Bill, which cover support for wheat, rice, corn, sorghum, barley, oats and cotton production (ICTSD 2004a; WTO 2004c). As many of these products are of export interest to African countries, the effect of this Blue Box enlargement is potentially disastrous. In addition, since the USA currently has no Blue Box subsidies, these payments will not just be exempt from reduction commitments, but in fact allow enjoying the benefits of an increase up to the 5 per cent threshold established in the July 2004 text.[2] This flexibility has the potential to reverse Brazil's success in the US Cotton case. Moreover, even though the Blue Box is considered a trade-distorting element of support, there is no commitment to reduce this support beyond the 5 per cent cap, which was a key demand by the G-20 prior to Cancun. In addition, the DWP provides more flexible treatment in relation to the cap, for a member with an 'exceptionally large percentage of its trade-distorting support in the Blue Box' (WTO 2004b: Para. 15). This will most likely give flexibility to the European Union (EU), and therefore essentially amounts to a continuation of the *de facto* 'reverse Special and Differential Treatment' granted under the AoA (Messerlin 2004). It is necessary to consider ways of minimizing the existing and potentially new negative impact that Blue Box support will have on African export interests.

Green Box

Subsidies provided under the Green Box are also problematic for African countries. Despite the fact that subsidies in this box must be decoupled, many Green Box programmes continue to distort trade by boosting farm revenues and the associated increase in production and depression of world prices (Watkins and von Braun 2003). This point has been established in the recent US Cotton case. The panel decision recognized the trade-distorting effects of certain Green Box policies, that can be seen as 'a radical challenge to the idea of decoupling that underpins the Green Box' (IPC 2004a: 4). The Green Box provisions are particularly important in relation to the discipline of US policy, as this involves 70 per cent of US domestic support (OECD 2004). For this reason it was necessary to have a cap on Green Box payments and a review of its trade-distorting elements and the development of 'tighter disciplines for elements of the Green Box through *inter alia* notification, surveillance and monitoring' (African Union 2004: 2). Instead, the DWP further entrenches the Green Box, without providing for any further discipline. The text includes neither a cap nor a commitment to reduce these subsidies, resulting in a significant loophole, permitting the increase in domestic support contrary to the Doha mandate.

The July 2004 text does foresee a revision of the criteria to ensure that Green Box measures actually are at the most minimally trade-distorting. It is of crucial African interest for this review to ensure that criteria are more reflective of the effect that many of these programmes have on production and prices. A surveillance mechanism for Green Box measures is also necessary (WTO 2004b: Para. 48).

De minimis

The *de minimis* clause currently provides an exemption for trade-distorting support up to 5 per cent of the total value of agricultural production and

10 per cent for developing countries. This important provision is used by nearly all developed countries, and is less used but yet still potentially important for developing countries (FAO 2003b).

The DWP establishes a mandate for negotiations to reduce these levels, but specifies that 'developing countries that allocate almost all *de minimis* programmes for subsistence and resource-poor farmers will be exempt'. The level of the reductions was not specified in the final DWP text, but previous drafts envisaged a 50 per cent cut (WTO 2003a). During the modalities phase there will be a need to secure significant general reductions, and moreover, to ensure that exemptions will be wide enough to protect African countries' own programmes, although it is clear that few African countries have the funds to provide significant support programmes. Botswana and Senegal are among the countries using the *de minimis* exception according to research by the UN Food and Agriculture Organization (FAO). The reduction of the *de minimis* level is of significance as a substantial part of support by developed countries is permitted under this exception. Consequently, significant reductions will lead to cuts in actual support levels, which is unlike many other provisions. In relation to the exemptions, the SDT limitation is potentially restrictive, as it may be difficult for some developing countries to meet the condition that the support must be channelled to subsistence and resource-poor farmers (Khor 2004). Although a similar SDT limitation is currently used for Amber Box subsidies, this does not seem to be restrictive (FAO 2003b).

Legal challenges to commodity subsidies

Dispute settlement is another area that is affecting the reform of the subsidy regimes of developed countries. There has been an increasing tendency towards legal challenges of commodity subsidies, partly as a result of the end of the peace clause that renders commodity-specific agricultural subsidies vulnerable to legal challenge (Steinberg and Josling 2003). Two prominent cases have been decided in 2004, where Brazil has succeeded in challenging the US cotton subsidies and EU sugar subsidies. Although this chapter cannot address the details of these findings, an assessment of the implications of the basic Panel finding is provided in the following paragraph.

In the cotton case, the panel ruled that subsidies granted to cotton farmers by the US government under certain programmes, such as marketing loans, export credits, commodity certificates and direct payments, depressed world market prices and were injurious to Brazil's trade interests. Similarly, in the sugar case, it is reported that the Panel found that the support measures by the EU for sugar produced for the internal market in fact acted as an export subsidy on the basis that this made it possible to export surplus sugar at below-cost prices (ICTSD 2004b and c).

Although it has been speculated previously that this legal vulnerability would indirectly help developing countries in forcing developed countries to commit themselves to further subsidy reductions, and to shift towards tariffs-and-decoupled-payments systems, the effect of the cotton case has been quite the opposite: a toughening of the US position on subsidy reduction. This case has 'forced [US] negotiators to insist on very specific language in the Doha Round Agreements' so as to provide legitimate foundation for payments under the 2002 Farm Bill (IPC 2004a).

The direct effect of these cases is also a mixed blessing for African countries. The cotton case is likely to be most beneficial, as it could encourage reduction of support to cotton growers, which is likely to increase the global cotton prices and benefit African exporters. However, it must be noted that reform of US domestic laws is not guaranteed as implementation is not fully guaranteed.[3] Moreover, expansion of the Blue Box has the potential to undermine any benefits of the ruling. Many of the payments in the USA deemed trade-distorting are among the counter-cyclical payments likely to be accommodated by the new Blue Box provisions (Raghavan 2004). This will enable the USA to increase support to its cotton growers, through the 5 per cent extra leeway granted by the Blue Box, rather than these payments being included in the AMS reduction calculations. However, the detrimental effect may be limited as Blue Box disciplines are to be negotiated to ensure that such payments will be less trade-distorting than AMS is (WTO 2004b: Para. 14).

The implications of the EU sugar decision are more complex. On the one hand, the sugar case has the benefit of providing legitimacy for the reform of such trade-distorting EU programmes, by securing member states acceptance of the Commission's proposal for reforming the sugar regime' (ICTSD 2004c). This reform will result in higher international market prices for sugar, which could help farmers in developing countries compete in international markets (Oxfam 2004a). On the other hand, for sugar producers in countries in Africa, the Caribbean and the Pacific belonging to the African Carribean and Pacific (ACP) group, the ruling will cause a major erosion of their traditional trade preferences, and undermine their export earnings. In addition, it is not clear that Africa will benefit from higher market prices. In fact it has been predicted that 'Brazil, already the world's number one sugar producer, will capture the lion's share of any new export opportunities opened up by the ruling' (ICTSD 2004c).

This raises the same broad dichotomy of interests as with the 'liberalization versus preference erosion' debate. Although the potential for price increases is important, and may be to the advantage of some developing countries, there is debate over Africa's ability to take advantage of these price increases. Although the major beneficiaries are likely to be larger and more competitive producing economies (in relation to sugar, this is likely to be Brazil, Australia, Thailand, the Philippines), smaller exporters may still receive significant benefits (ILEAP 2003). Nonetheless, African countries must ensure that they are in a position to take advantage of the removal of such distortions in commodity markets, by addressing the supply-side constraints. In this regard, the importance of domestic policies and actions must not be underestimated. Domestic policies such as investment in infrastructure (e.g. in transportation and telecommunications), well-functioning credit and other input markets (seeds, fertilizers), and competitive markets in distribution can all help to ensure that Africans will benefit from trade liberalization (Messerlin 2004). Such projects clearly require additional resources, which could potentially be raised through adjustment support schemes (Werth and Lee 2004).

Legal issues outside the AoA

Another important issue raised by these legal challenges to commodity subsidies is in the potential constraints for small developing countries to participate or benefit from such litigation in the future. It is important to consider issues of remedies, proof and evidence in order to ensure that those countries will not be in a disadvantage in this process. In relation to remedies, reform of the current Dispute Settlement Understanding (DSU) remedy provisions is necessary to ensure that such countries are able to effectively enforce WTO decisions, through the establishment of monetary compensation as an SDT remedy (ILEAP 2003) or alternative retaliation schemes (Bagwell *et al.* 2003). In addition, it would be beneficial to reform the burden of proof in case subsidies are challenged by developing countries. For example Stiglitz calls for 'a heavier burden [to be] placed on those claiming that particular forms of subsidy are not trade-distorting' (Stiglitz and Charlton 2004). This could be achieved through a more effective Green Box monitoring mechanism. Such a monitoring mechanism, foreshadowed in Para. 48 of the DWP, could put more pressure on Green Box users, provided there is improved transparency on such measures. Alternatively, consideration should be given to reform of Subsidy and Countervailing Measures provisions, which could enable small developing countries to prove more easily that certain subsidies are causing serious prejudice to their economies. For example, African countries could consider pushing for the reinstatement of the 'deemed serious prejudice' provisions that expired in 1999, which would make it easier for members to challenge commodity subsidies in the future. This provision – Article 6.1(a) of the AoA, Domestic Support Commitments – relieved complainants of proving serious prejudice for subsidies amounting to more than 5 per cent of the value of production. These issues will become increasingly important if it turns out to be correct that the AoA reform founded in the DWP will be inadequate to discipline the agricultural subsidies of the USA and the EU.[4] The reinstatement of Article 6.1(a) of the AoA has been proposed by Canada in 2003, on the basis that these provisions conferred an evidentiary advantage to complainants.

Cotton initiative

In May 2003, Benin, Burkina Faso, Chad and Mali requested a complete phasing out of support measures for the production and exports of cotton, and the establishment of a transitional compensatory mechanism to off-set income losses of cotton producers in least-developed countries (LDCs) while cotton subsidies are being phased out (WTO 2003b). The DWP includes a reference to the Cotton initiative but no significant achievements have been made on this issue. During intense negotiations in the lead up to the July 2004 meetings, the proponents had given up on their original demand that this be dealt with as a stand-alone issue. Importantly, the proponents' request for a 'fast-track' timetable for cotton subsidy reduction was maintained. The DWP acknowledged that the issue must be addressed ambitiously, expeditiously and specifically, and established a subcommittee on cotton. However the text provides no guarantees in relation to fast-track cotton subsidy reduction. It is clear that the product-specific caps on AMS support and the associated reductions (WTO 2004b: Para. 9) will not be effective because US payments can still continue under the new Blue Box – albeit in a less trade-distorting fashion – or the largely untouched Green Box. Therefore proponents will have to continue pushing for fast-track reductions, potentially within a wider commodity fast-track approach, and may wish to consider further pursuing the idea of a monitoring mechanism. The EU has already decided to 'establish a mechanism to monitor the impact of its cotton support and the reform on international cotton production and trade' (EC 2004). A similar mechanism with an international focus would be beneficial, and could potentially be established within the WTO research division.

Export competition

An important achievement of the DWP is the commitment to abolish export subsidies. Despite this achievement, the timetable for their elimination is still not agreed, and consequently future negotiations will be crucial. The elimination of export subsidies is likely to benefit some African countries, particularly producers of products that are highly subsidized by the EU, including sugar, dairy and meat products (WTO 2003c). For a few food importers, there could be an increase in costs to consumers as a result of subsidy withdrawal, which must be addressed in line with the Marrakesh Decision on Measures Concerning the Possible Negative Effects of the Reform Programme on Least-Developed and Net Food-Importing Developing Countries. From the African perspective, however, it will be important to ensure that the elimination occurs at a very near date, or at least for those products which are of particular importance for Africa.

Language on export credit and food aid programmes is less clear. Although the DWP promises to end the trade-distorting elements of these measures, it is unclear how this will be enforced. African countries must continue to push for strong language in these areas. Provisions in relation to state trading enterprises (STEs) are also important for African countries. The main concern is that the deregulation of STEs might be disastrous for developing countries since STEs stabilize prices and food supply and play a critical role in ensuring food security (Focusweb 2004). Hence it is necessary to introduce explicit SDT for developing country STEs. Despite this omission, it still may be possible for developing countries to push for longer implementation periods in relation to STE deregulation. In addition, the issue of 'the future use of monopoly powers' will be subject to further negotiation, which will be of interest to Africa.

Market access

Market access has been an area of focus for most WTO members. For the Africa group, the goals are to ensure increased market access, reduced tariff peaks and tariff escalation, while reserving the right to high tariffs on Special Products and establishing a Special Safeguard Mechanism (SSM) (WTO 2003d).

The DWP outlines a single tiered formula approach with cuts being made from final bound levels, which includes provisions for the different tariff structures of developed and developing countries, with exemption of LDCs from cuts, 'differential provisions for developing country members' and 'deeper cuts in higher tariffs' (WTO 2004b). The framework does not, however, provide any details as to bands, thresholds, tariff reduction formulas or tariff caps.

The formula negotiations are of vital importance, and will determine the effectiveness of increasing market access. Previous Chairmen's texts have been problematic as they are unlikely to achieve the aims of reductions in tariff peaks for a number of reasons. The 'average-cut' formulation is particularly problematic (ILEAP 2004a). Briefly, an average cut can be achieved by cutting very low tariffs, without changing the peak tariffs at all.

Although the July 2004 text states that 'substantial improvements in market access will be achieved for all products' (Para. 29, point 3), it is unclear how this will be guaranteed or how effective this will be in practice, especially if expansion of tariff rate quotas (TRQ) is the envisaged solution. The result might be a lack of improvement in real market access. For this reason, it is important that the formula does not include such loopholes. In addition, an effective tariff cap, limiting the exceptions that will be available will be necessary for African objectives to be realized in the market access pillar (WTO 2004b: Para. 30). Without an effective tariff cap, there is no guarantee that tariff peaks will be avoided.

Other important issues for Africa in this area include NTBs and duty-free access for LDCs. In relation to NTBs, it is recognized that trade restrictions governed by the agreements on Sanitary and Phytosanitary Standards (SPSs) and Technical Barriers to Trade (TBTs) have the potential to undermine market access gains for Africa (African Union 2004). A study by the FAO (2003b) of the UN noted:

> It is important that non-tariff barriers such as SPS and TBT are transparent if African developing countries are not to be denied access to developed markets. With their scarce resources, African developing countries are vulnerable to the differing, duplicative testing standards or discriminative requirements in developed markets. Even if they are not a complete deterrent, they still burden exporters with additional costs they can ill afford.

However, the issue of regulatory barriers has not been addressed in the DWP. Similarly, the Programme leaves the issue of duty-free and quota-free access for LDCs 'under negotiation', which means that this issue of crucial important to LDC export-led development is still open.

Preference erosion

The issue of preferences is important for many African countries. For countries that benefit from preferences, market-access benefits are undermined as tariffs are reduced. There have been various attempts at assessing and quantifying the problem of preference erosion (Alexandraki and Lankes 2004; Subramanian 2003). Most studies suggest the losses will be small, with significant effects predicted in relation to the sugar and banana regimes.[5]

Many developing countries have expressed their desire for a mechanism to compensate those losing from preference erosion. However, there has been minimal progress on this issue within the WTO framework and no further advances in the DWP, based on the assumption that this is essentially a problem for the International Monetary Fund (IMF) and The World Bank rather than the WTO. The most positive response to the issue has been the establishment by the IMF of the Trade Integration Mechanism (TIM), in March 2004. This was designed to 'mitigate concerns that implementation of WTO agreements might give rise to temporary balance of payments shortfalls'. There is concern that this mechanism will not be effective for a number of reasons: it provides no additional funding beyond existing IMF facilities, and relies on standard IMF criteria rather than being directly tied to a country's total loss from preference erosion. In addition, the funds are on standard IMF terms (i.e. loans rather than grants) thereby likely to increase debt burdens (Page 2004). Alternative methods of compensatory financing designed to address the long-term problem of commodity dependence is imperative. It is important to note that Para. 44 of the DWP also refers to Para. 16 of the previous Harbinson text, which provides for assistance in diversifying away from commodities subject to certain preferences.

Sensitive Products

According to the DWP all countries will be able to designate 'an appropriate number' (to be negotiated) of Sensitive Products to which the formula will not apply. This loophole was demanded by the EU and other G-10 members. Although 'substantial improvement in market access' will still be required, there is real concern that this provision will continue to prevent or limit market access of agricultural exports and potential exports (Khor 2004). Sensitive Products are likely to include highly protected sectors and those most vulnerable to import competition. For example, developed countries are likely to include sugar, dairy products, beef meat, cereals and cotton on their list (Peters and Vanzetti 2004). A major concern is that many of these products are of export interest to African countries, thereby severely undermining the effectiveness of market access improvements.

The original Groser draft envisaged an extremely wide exception, available to a number of tariff lines approximately equal to those with out-of-quota tariff rates (WTO 2004a). This is a large allowance for flexibility, estimated to cover 20 per cent of tariff lines and 55 per cent of production in developed countries (De Gorter and Hranaiova 2004; The World Bank 2004). Although the final July 2004 text is less detailed, there is a risk that the outcome will be similar to that intended in the original draft. In addition, there is doubt as to the effectiveness of TRQ expansion as a method of increasing market access. TRQ expansion may be problematic for a number of reasons: lack of transparency, poor fill rates, discriminatory administration of quotas and lack of due process. For these reasons a more restrictive definition of Sensitive Products than foreshadowed in the Groser draft will be required for the final agreement.[6]

Special and Differential Treatment

There are competing views on the extent to which trade barriers such as tariffs and safeguards can be effective in addressing African food security, livelihood security and rural development concerns. Some argue that arrangements such as Special Products SSM are simply veils for basic protectionism, whereas others warn about the negative potential welfare effects of these mechanisms. Messerlin argues, 'The proposal for a special safeguard for agriculture is a bad idea for three reasons' (Messerlin 2004). However, several African countries (Botswana, Kenya, Mauritius, Nigeria, Tanzania, Uganda and Zimbabwe, included in the SP/SSM Alliance or G-33) have been vehement supporters of the Special Products/SSM proposals. The Africa Group has also given general support to these concepts (WTO 2001). Although both concepts were included in the DWP, the lack of specificity in the text means that a great deal of negotiating effort is still required to ensure that these mechanisms will effectively address African concerns.

Special Products

The DWP confirms that developing countries would be able to designate 'an appropriate number' of Special Products, based on criteria of food security, livelihood security and rural development needs. The criteria and treatment of these products will be specified through further negotiations, which will be of great interest to African countries. Although this is designed to be a measure of SDT, it is interesting to note that the selection is likely to be limited by 'criteria', unlike the selection of 'Sensitive Products' that are left to self-selection by the member country. The selection of Special Products will be a complex task that will need to take into account a variety of considerations, including: domestic conditions such as rural and urban poverty indicators; domestic policy, such as poverty reduction and development plans; and effectiveness indicators – involving an assessment of country- and sector-specific applied and bound tariff rates (ILEAP forthcoming). Flexibility in a Special Products arrangement as currently proposed will likely be of real benefit to only a limited number of African countries and products, due to the current tariff structures. The modality of Special Products will not be useful where there is already a large gap between applied and bound tariff rates. Thus, African countries must be careful not to over-invest negotiating capacity on this issue. There are also a number of potential legal constraints including the potential for legal challenges to the selection of Special Products, and current legal restrictions on the increase in tariff up to bound, which have the potential to hinder the effectiveness of the Special Products modality unless these issues are addressed in future negotiations (ILEAP forthcoming).

Special Safeguard Mechanism

Although the DWP confirms that an SSM will be established for use by developing countries, the text gives no details as to how the SSM will function. Further negotiations will be critical, as the basic concepts of product coverage, trigger mechanisms and the functioning of the mechanism will all determine the effectiveness of the mechanism for African countries. On product coverage, it is important that a broad approach is taken: the SSM should not be limited to food crops that are important for food security. Instead, it should be made available for all products, including those selected as Special Products. ILEAP research highlights the need for a complementary approach, based on the distinct functions of the two mechanisms, and the inadequate protection offered by the Special Products modality alone (ILEAP forthcoming). It is essential to link the eligibility of products for the SSM to levels of bound or applied tariffs.

Services

In contrast to the agriculture negotiations, there has been little movement in the area of services. In fact, the DWP and Doha mandate contain no specific aims beyond the establishment of new deadlines (May 2005) for revised offers. African countries are not participating in this process to a large extent, as most of them have not submitted initial requests to their trading partners. Nor have they been able to formulate their initial offer of liberalization under the General Agreement on Trade in Services (GATS). In general, the areas of potential interest for African countries are in the temporary movement of labour (Mode 4), some labour-intensive sectors such as tourism, and infrastructure-related services such as telecommunications, and financial and transport services. Regarding the latter three types of services, these countries may not have export interests but these services are crucial for enhancing competitiveness. African countries have an interest in participating in GATS negotiations in order to consider the option of further liberalization in backbone or other key commercial or social sectors to spur development and improve competitiveness, and to explore to what extent such offers in market access and national treatment could be traded against new concessions to be made by their trading partners in areas of specific export interest to African countries. In this bargaining exercise, African LDCs should take as a key reference the Special Modalities for LDCs under GATS, agreed just prior to Cancun.

With respect to Mode 4, the potential gains are high, as this is one of the most restricted areas of services, while being an area of comparative advantage for Africa due to the lower costs of skilled labour and of labour-intensive sectors. Worker remittances are already a significant source of income for developing countries, and this could increase if further liberalization occurs. An increase in the number of temporary workers by 3 per cent in developed countries could contribute 160 billion US dollars to the total income of developing countries (Winters 2002). Also, the demographic momentum in developed countries is providing a window of opportunity for creating equilibrium between global supply and demand for labour. A challenge for African countries is to negotiate improved commitments in sectors that are of interest to them. Such an exercise will require country- and sector-specific analyses to determine areas where there are genuine reasons for limiting entry, as well as actions in favour of alleviating supply constraints in particular.

Trade facilitation

The DWP also launched negotiations on trade facilitation, one of the four Singapore Issues that had been opposed by African countries at Cancun. The aim of the trade facilitation negotiations is more transparency, efficiency and procedural uniformity of cross-border transportation of goods. The DDA negotiating mandate in trade facilitation covers GATT Articles V, Freedom of Transit, Article VIII, Fees and Formalities Connected with Importation and Exportation, and Article X, Publication and Administration of Trade Regulations, as well as provisions and obligations such as on customs valuation, pre-shipment inspection, rules of origin or TBT.

Properly negotiated, African countries have much to gain, as trade facilitation-related activities represent a large share of trade costs in Africa, and these limitations restrict the expansion and growth that Africa can achieve as a result of liberalization (Mwalwanda 2003). However there are a number of concerns, including the high potential costs of implementation, and the question whether it is appropriate to involve the WTO dispute settlement system – as opposed to non-binding guidelines – for this area. The DWP addresses some of these developing country concerns, specifically in relation to implementation costs (Para. 4) and technical assistance (Para. 6). Most importantly, the text includes a caveat that exempts developing countries from implementation of the final agreement if support and assistance for the required infrastructure are missing or if they continue to lack the necessary capacity.

Market access for non-agricultural products

From an African perspective, NAMA is a less important issue than market access for agricultural products, as the current structure of developed country protection is less restrictive and less complex. Although tariffs are relatively low for manufactured products, some highly protected sectors exist and it has been noted that 'tariffs are biased against sectors of export interest to developing countries, and Non-Tariff Barriers (NTBs) are frequent and concentrated in such sectors' (UNCTAD 2004). Areas of strong protection include: textiles, clothing, fish, rubber and leather goods (Page 2004). Therefore, it is in the interest of African countries to improve market access in these sectors as well as to diminish tariff escalation and specific duties.

On the defensive side, African countries are concerned with respect to the impact of the formula on their industrial tariffs, unless appropriate provision for less than full reciprocity is introduced. As a consequence of the focus on agriculture, little progress was made on NAMA in the DWP. The July 2004 text outlines 'initial elements for future work on modalities' based on the Derbez text presented at the WTO Ministerial of Cancun. As developing countries expressed serious concerns about the Derbez text, the DWP recognizes that 'additional negotiations are required to reach agreement on the specifics of these elements'. In particular, negotiations on the formula, the treatment of unbound tariffs, developing country flexibilities, the sectoral component and preferences remain contentious.

The DWP provides for the continuation of work on a non-linear formula based on bound rates, which many developing countries believe contradicts the principle of less than full reciprocity set out in the DDA. This formula requires deeper cuts for higher tariffs, and consequently would result in deeper cuts to be made by developing countries that have relatively high bound tariff rates (UNCTAD 2004). With respect to unbound tariffs, the DWP establishes tariff reductions based on applied rates, which may have the consequence of locking in low rates for African countries, including LDCs.[7] With respect to the sectoral tariff component, the key issue will be whether the participation will be mandatory or voluntary. The DWP (Para. 7) notes that participation by all in the initiative would be important, thus implying that this could be voluntary.

Preference erosion will be another major concern, with the DWP reaffirming the importance of this issue. African countries will need to pursue both trade solutions and development instruments, focusing on adjustment support and assistance in building sustainable supply capacities (UNCTAD 2004). Finally, negotiations on NTBs in the NAMA Negotiating Group will be crucial to effectively improve African market access.

Conclusion

The DWP provides an important foundation for the future DDA negotiations. The Doha Round is of crucial importance for African development and integration into the international trading system. Many issues of African interest are addressed in the DWP, albeit with varying degrees of generality and ambiguity. In order to further progress on these issues, it is crucial to build on the DWP and to articulate provisions that are beneficial for development. The DWP does not as yet contain a clear and binding development 'deal'. Therefore, it is key for African countries to obtain significant improvements on development provisions. In agriculture, the first objective should be to effectively discipline support by developed countries and pry open their markets, to ensure that systemic imbalances in the current AoA are addressed, and to ensure that hard-won SDT flexibilities are developed in a way that protects the policy space required for the implementation of African development strategies. With respect to NAMA, services and trade facilitation, African countries should play a more pro-active role, requiring further analysis of both competitive and sensitive sectors for African countries.

Notes

1 The views expressed in this chapter are personal and should not be attributed to ILEAP.
2 The 5 per cent threshold is established in Para. 15 of the DWP. It should be kept in mind that there will be reduction of *de minimis* which could off-set this new flexibility – at least in terms of overall volumes.
3 The USA has not complied with the WTO rulings in the Foreign Sales Corporation FSC and Byrd Amendment cases, and according to commentators it is unlikely that the Byrd Amendment will be repealed before 2006, despite the EU's ability to retaliate with tariffs up to 150 million US dollars per year (The *Economist* 2004).
4 This 5 per cent threshold has been well and truly surpassed for many of the US support programmes. In fact the following commodities receive support at a level higher than 20 per cent of the value of production: sugar, rice, peanuts, soybeans, tobacco, dairy and cotton. Calculations based on WTO 2004c.
5 The estimation is for an average loss of less than 2 per cent of exports for LDCs and between 0.5 and 1.2 per cent of total exports for middle-income countries. Bananas and sugar are expected to account for more than three-quarters of the losses of preference erosion. See Alexandraki and Lankes (2004) and Subramanian (2003).

6 For example Africa could still challenge the foundations of the Sensitive Products' concept in future negotiations, on the basis of the incoherence between the flexibilities offered to developed countries (with no criteria with which to comply) and the more strict discipline on developing countries selection (which is likely to be based on criteria).

7 The DWP establishes tariff bindings at two times the applied tariff rate, Para. 5, and includes LDCs, Para. 9.

Bibliography

African Union (2004) 'Kigali consensus on the post-Cancun Doha work programme', AU/TD/MIN/Decl.1 (II), Annex, Addis Abbaba: African Union.

Alexandraki, K. and Lankes, H. (2004) 'Estimating the impact of preference erosion on Middle-Income Countries', IMF Working Paper, Washington, DC: IMF.

Bagwell, K., Mavroidis, P. and Staiger, R. (2003) 'The case for auctioning counter-measures in the WTO', NBER Working Paper No. 9920, Washington, DC: NBER.

Chandrasekhar, C. (2004) 'WTO and agriculture: once more with vengeance', Agriculture Framework Analysis, New Delhi: International Development Economics Associates (IDEAS). Available online at http://www.networkideas.org/news/jul2004/print/prnt270704_WTO_Agriculture.htm (accessed 14 October 2005).

EC (2004) 'EC Press Release', 5 May. Available online, at http://europa.eu.int/comm/agriculture/external/wto/press/ipcotton.pdf (accessed 14 October 2005).

Economist, The (2004) 'Byrd-brained: America's Congress runs afoul of the World Trade Organization, again', 2 September.

FAO (2003a) 'Market access for developing countries of Africa – the reality', AGSF Occasional Paper No. 1, Rome: FAO. Available online at http://www.fao.org/ag/ags/subjects/en/agmarket/access.doc (accessed 14 October 2005).

FAO (2003b) 'WTO agreement on agriculture: the implementation experience – developing country case studies', *Commodity Policy and Projections Service*, Commodities and Trade Division, Rome: FAO.

Focusweb (2004) 'Makings of a round that will be catastrophic for the poor', Bangkok: Focus on the Global South. Available online at http://www.focusweb.org/main/html/Article390.html (accessed 17 October 2005).

Gorter, H. de and Hranaiova, J. (2004) 'Quota administration methods: economics and effects with trade liberalization', in M. Ingco and J. Nash (eds) *Agriculture and the WTO: Creating a Trading System for Development*, Washington, DC: The World Bank and Oxford University Press.

Hart, C. and Beghin, J. (2004) 'Rethinking agricultural domestic support under the World Trade Organization', Briefing Paper 04-BP43, Ames IA: Center for Agricultural and Rural Development (CARD) and Food and Agricultural Policy Research Institute (FAPRI). Development of IOWA state university (draft copy on file with author).

Hoekman, B., Ng, F. and Olarreaga, M. (2002) 'Reducing agriculture tariffs versus domestic support: what's more important for developing countries?', World Bank Working Paper No. 2918, Washington, DC: The World Bank.

IATP (2004) 'The Framework text on agriculture – worth rejecting', Minneapolis MN: Institute for Agriculture and Trade Policy. Available online at http://www.tradeobservatory.org/library.cfm?reflD=36869 (accessed 17 October 2005).

ICTSD (2004a) 'How significant is the latest WTO deal?', *Bridges, Weekly Trade News Digest* 8 (7), Geneva: International Centre for Trade and Sustainable Development.

ICTSD (2004b) 'WTO releases cotton report; US vows to appeal', *Bridges Weekly Trade News Digest* 8 (29), Geneva: International Centre for Trade and Sustainable Development.

ICTSD (2004c) 'Sugar subsidies: Brazil scores again', *Bridges Weekly Trade News Digest* 8 (27), Geneva: International Centre for Trade and Sustainable Development.

ILEAP (2003) 'Agriculture – modalities', Negotiating Policy Brief No. 2, Toronto: International Lawyers and Economists Against Poverty (ILEAP). Available online at http://www.ileapinitiative.com (accessed 17 October 2005).

ILEAP (2004a) 'The framework for market access negotiations provided by the Derbez Draft', Advisory Brief No. 1, Toronto: ILEAP. Available online at http://www.ileapinitiative.com (accessed 17 October 2005).

ILEAP (2004b) 'A comparative reading of the groser draft text on agriculture from a development perspective', Negotiation Note No. 4, Toronto: ILEAP. Available online at http://www.ileapinitiative.com (accessed 17 October 2005).

ILEAP (2004c) 'Legal issues in relation to financial compensation under the cotton Initiative', Negotiating Policy Brief No. 3, Toronto: ILEAP. Available online at http://www.ileapinitiative.com (accessed 17 October 2005).

ILEAP (forthcoming) 'The Special Products modality: an evaluation', Toronto: ILEAP.

IPC (2004a) 'The cotton panel: implications for US agricultural policy and the WTO negotiations', IPC roundtable discussion seminar proceedings, Washington, DC/Brussels: International Food and Agricultural Trade Policy Council. Available online at http://www.cottonafrica.com/downloads/WTO%20and %20Subsidies.pdf (accessed 17 October 2005).

IPC (2004b) 'Agricultural Trade Council praises Doha Agricultural Framework as sound basis for moving forward', Press Release, Washington, DC Brussels: International Food and Agricultural Trade Policy Council.

Khor, M. (2004) 'Preliminary comments on the WTO's Geneva July decision', Penang: Third World Network.

Messerlin, P. (2004) 'Forging a deal on agricultural trade reform: a scenario paper', Paper Presented at the conference on *Breaking the Deadlock on Agricultural Reform and Development: How Could a Leaders' Level G20 Make a Difference?'* Oxford: Oxford University.

Mwalwanda, C. (2003) 'Trade facilitation in a multilateral framework: challenges for Africa', Addis Abbaba: UNECA.

OECD (2004) 'Agricultural policies in OECD countries at a glance', Paris: OECD.

Oxfam (2004a) 'Dumping on the world: how EU sugar policies hurt poor countries', Oxfam Briefing Paper No. 61, Oxford: Oxfam.

Oxfam (2004b) 'Dumping: the beginning of the end? implications of the ruling in the Brazil/US cotton dispute', Oxfam Briefing paper No. 64, Oxford: Oxfam.

Oxfam (2004c) 'One minute to midnight: will WTO negotiations in July deliver a meaningful agreement?', Oxfam Briefing paper No. 65, Oxford: Oxfam.

Page, S. (2004) 'Principal issues in the Doha negotiations, assessing the poverty impact of the Doha negotiations', London: Overseas Development Institute (Study funded by DFID).

Peters, R. and Vanzetti, D. (2004) 'Shifting sands: searching for a compromise in the WTO negotiations on agriculture', Policy Issues in International Trade and Commodities Study Series No. 23. Available online at http://www.unctad.org/en/docs//itcdtab23_en.pdf (accessed 17 October 2005).

Raghavan, C. (2004) 'Agriculture framework, an asymmetric Doha-minus', Southcentre on-line commentary, 19 July. Available online at http://www.twnside.org.sg/title2/5618b.htm (accessed 17 October 2005).

Steinberg R. and Josling, T. (2003) 'When the peace ends: the vulnerability of EC and US agricultural subsidies to WTO legal challenge', *Journal of International Economic Law*, Vol. 6, No. 2, pp. 369–417.

Stiglitz, J., and Charlton, A., with the Initiative for Policy Dialogue (IDP) (2004) 'The development round of trade negotiations in the aftermath of Cancun', a report for the Commonwealth Secretariat. Available online at http://www.thecommonwealth.org. (accessed 17 October 2005).

Subramanian, A. (2003) 'Financing of losses from preferences erosion', paper prepared for the WTO, WT/TF/COH/14.

Sutherland, P. (2004) 'Beware cost of failure in the Doha talks', *Financial Times*, 8 July.

UNCTAD (2004) 'Review of developments and issues in the post-Doha work programme of particular concern to developing countries: a post UNCTAD XI perspective', TD/B/51/4, Geneva: UNCTAD.

Watkins, K. (2004) 'WTO negotiations on agriculture: problems and ways ahead', paper presented at *Strategic Dialogue on Agriculture, Trade Negotiations, Poverty and Sustainability* organized by ICTSD and IIED in Windsor, UK, July 2004. Available online at http://www.ictsd.org/dlogue/2004-07-14/2004-07-14-docu.htm (accessed 17 October 2005).

Watkins, K. and Braun, J. von (2003) 'Time to stop dumping on the world's poor' in *2002–2003 IPFRI Annual Report*, Washington, DC: IFPRI.

Werth, A. and Lee, B. (2004), 'Embedding a pro-poor approach in agriculture trade reform', paper presented at *Strategic Dialogue on Agriculture, Trade Negotiations, Poverty and Sustainability* organized by ICTSD and IIED in Windsor, UK. Available online at http://www.ictsd.org/dlogue/2004-07-14/2004-07-14-docu.htm (accessed 17 October 2005).

Winters, A.L. (2002) 'The economic implication of liberalizing Mode 4 trade', Paper for the Joint WTO-WB Symposium, Geneva.

World Bank, The (2004) 'Market access in agriculture: beyond the blender', Trade Note No. 16, Washington, DC: The World Bank.

WTO (2001) 'WTO African group: joint proposal on the negotiations on agriculture', G/AG/NG/W/142, Geneva: WTO.

WTO (2003a) 'Harbinson text', TN/AG/W/1/Rev.1, Geneva: WTO.

WTO (2003b) 'Submission by Benin, Burkino Faso, Chad and Mali', TN/AG/GEN/4, Geneva: WTO.

WTO (2003c) 'EU notification to the WTO on export subsidies', G/AG/N/EEC/44, Geneva: WTO.

WTO (2003d) 'Consolidated African Union/ACP/LDC position on agriculture', WT/MIN(03)/W/17, Geneva: WTO.

WTO (2004a) 'Groser draft July framework', JOB(04)/96, Geneva: WTO.

WTO (2004b) 'Doha Work Programme, decision adopted by the General Council', WT/L/579, Geneva: WTO.

WTO (2004c) 'US WTO notification', G/AG/N/USA/51, Geneva: WTO.

9 Towards a development round

Pitou van Dijck and Gerrit Faber

Introduction

The Doha Development Agenda (DDA) holds the promise of supporting reforms of trade policies that will not only bring immediate welfare gains for developing and developed countries, but enhance overall growth and contribute to the alleviation of poverty. In an optimistic Doha scenario, Anderson (2004) calculated that every dollar spent on restructuring, retraining and social safety nets, required to facilitate the reduction of trade barriers and subsidies by half in all member countries of the World Trade Organization (WTO), would have a benefits–costs ratio of 24.3 for all participating countries and even 37.9 for developing countries. However, these high returns do not guarantee that the necessary steps will be taken to make the promises come true.

The studies collected in this volume show that many contested issues and proposals may seriously hamper progress in realizing a final package of concessions and commitments in support of development and poverty alleviation. The design of a package that is at the same time acceptable to all WTO members, is a complex and delicate task, and there is a serious risk that the ultimate mechanism to produce these beneficial effects – improved market access – will not get sufficient room.

In this concluding chapter we shall bring together the main findings on potential gains for developing countries that may be generated by a successful DDA as well as the main obstacles to the realization of such a result, as identified by the authors of the previous chapters. This may help to delineate the package of possible outcomes of the DDA and to formulate a set of critical conditions for a final agreement of the Doha Round that would do justice to the ambitions as laid down at the onset of the negotiations.

Modelling concessions for development

Theoretical analysis and general equilibrium models show that developing countries potentially have much to gain from trade liberalization. After many decades during which more inward-orientated types of development strategies were pursued, most developing countries have been liberalizing their economies by, *inter alia*, reducing non-tariff barriers (NTBs) to trade, binding import tariffs and cutting the levels of bound and particularly applied tariff rates substantially. Nearly all developing countries have locked in their unilateral liberalization policies by concessions made during several rounds of the General Agreement on Tariffs and Trade (GATT), and more recently in the WTO. Moreover, protection has been cut further in many countries by their participation in a spaghetti bowl of numerous preferential trade agreements (PTAs) among themselves as well as with developed countries. Although country-specific experiences differ widely and generalizations are hard to make, nearly all developing countries have in common that their economies have been liberalized significantly since the start of the Uruguay Round.

So far, support by developing countries for further liberalization in the DDA negotiations has been piecemeal and strongly conditional. With trepidation, many countries view that abstract long-term gains may come at high short-term costs in terms of loss of possibilities for national industrial policies, loss of preferential margins, high restructuring costs and resource-intensive regulatory harmonization in areas of standardization and trade facilitation.

To help understand the different positions of countries in the current round of negotiations, the general equilibrium model as applied by Kym Anderson *et al.* in Chapter 2 of this volume shows the impact of complete, global trade reform in developed and developing countries and regions, and of six Doha liberalization scenarios, involving different packages of concessions. Four of these scenarios focus on liberalization of agriculture only, reflecting the crucial role of this sector in the DDA.

Clearly, the model shows that full liberalization of global merchandise trade – which is definitely not on the DDA – would generate a much more substantial result in terms of welfare gains, as measured by additional over-all real income and change in factor prices, than any of the alternative and less ambitious 'realistic' Doha scenarios for cutting applied tariff rates that have been run with the model. Full liberalization would generate 287 billion US dollars in welfare gains in 2015, two-thirds of which (201 billion US dollars) would benefit developed countries. Percentage-wise, this would involve a rise in real income in 2015 relative to the baseline income in 2001 of 0.6 per cent in developed countries, 0.8 per cent in developing countries and 1.2 per cent when applying the WTO definition of developing countries. The model findings indicate that all developing countries would enjoy net positive effects of worldwide full liberalization and that, measured percentage-wise in terms of the baseline scenario, gains would be largest in the Middle East and North Africa (1.2), Sub-Saharan Africa (1.1) and Latin America and the Caribbean (1.0), respectively. These results are generated notwithstanding strong negative terms-of-trade effects experienced by the overall group of developing countries.

The relatively small size of the welfare effects of liberalization, as generated by the model even in the case of the most ambitious of all possible outcomes, is presumably related to the essentially static nature of the model, notwithstanding some dynamic features. A more comprehensive and accurate incorporation of dynamic factors including a realistic savings–accumulation path could generate more substantial gains from trade than the current model does, as suggested by Michiel Keyzer in Chapter 3 of the volume. Moreover, the model focuses exclusively on the potential impact of liberalization measures in agriculture and manufactures, bypassing other elements of the DDA such as services, foreign direct investment (FDI), trade-related aspects of intellectual property rights (TRIPS) and trade facilitation, which have the potential to far outweigh the impact of reducing trade barriers in food products, as Joseph Francois puts it in Chapter 4 of this volume.

The model does show country-wise the impact of full liberalization on real factor prices by differentiating income effects for unskilled and skilled wages and costs for users of capital and land. The results indicate that in developing countries the remuneration of unskilled labour and land, as measured in US dollars, would increase more than remuneration of skilled workers, and even more so as compared to capital. To the extent that poverty is concentrated among the unskilled and farmers, this indicates a positive contribution of liberalization to poverty reduction. At the same time, however, the model is not capable to measure welfare effects on the poor directly, as observed by Michiel Keyzer.

Welfare gains are due to efficiency gains and changes in the international terms of trade for each country. The more domestic protection is reduced, the larger potential efficiency gains may be; the more protection in potential export markets is reduced, the more terms-of-trade effects may contribute to overall welfare gains; and the more prices of imports rise due to liberalization, the larger negative terms-of-trade effects for a country may be.

Terms-of-trade effects appear to be strongly positive for some developed countries such as the USA, Japan, Australia and New Zealand, and a group of developing countries including Hong Kong and Singapore, Brazil, Argentina, and Thailand. They are strongly negative in the case of India, China, the Middle East and North Africa, Mexico and in some but not all countries in Sub-Saharan African (SSA). So, although full liberalization contributes to welfare in all developing countries, be it to different degrees, the impact of international price increases due to worldwide liberalization may differ strongly between countries and even within groups of countries like the group of least-developed countries (LDCs) and the G-20.

Remarkably, the gains from full liberalization of 90 billion US dollars in developing countries are exactly as much due to liberalization in their own group as they are to liberalization in developed countries. Put differently, the less countries liberalize, the more limited their gains from trade will be.

Clearly, the model shows the critical role of reform of agricultural policy for the outcomes to be significant from the perspective of global welfare and more specifically from a developmental point of view. At the level of the world economy, 62 per cent of the 287 billion US dollars gains from full liberalization are due to agricultural reform, rather evenly distributed between the effects of liberalization of the agricultural sectors in high-income and the groups of low and middle-income countries. This should not come as a surprise because of the high level of import protection in agriculture as compared to the non-agriculture sectors: the average applied import tariff rate in agriculture in high, middle and low-income countries in 2001 is 16.0, 16.5 and 22.2 per cent respectively. Indeed, improved market access in agriculture generates the overwhelming share of the liberalization effect in that sector, with subsidy cutting contributing relatively little to welfare in developing countries, taken as a group.

In all probability, the results of the negotiations on the DDA will ultimately be less comprehensive than in the full liberalization scenario presented earlier. For that reason the study by Kym Anderson *et al.* includes six scenarios, all starting from the actual pre-simulation tariff levels.

When comparing the impact of several Doha scenarios on tariff cutting for agricultural products it is found that the world average applied tariff rate is cut substantially from 15.2 per cent in the pre-simulation situation to 10.0 per cent in the Tiered Formula scenario and to 10.3 per cent in the Proportional scenario, implying an average worldwide cut in tariff rates of approximately 34 per cent, of about 45 per cent in developed countries, 15 per cent in middle-income countries and 6 per cent in low-income countries. Moreover, it appears that the difference in impact between the Tiered Formula scenario and the Proportional scenario is only limited. However, inclusion of special regulations and exemptions for Sensitive Products with or without a cap for maximal tariff rates would significantly reduce the tariff-cutting impact of concessions. In the Sensitive+Cap scenario the average applied tariff rate for agricultural products in developed countries would be cut from 15.9 per cent in the pre-simulation situation to 11.5 per cent, in middle-income countries from 12.1 to 11.2 per cent and in low-income countries from 22.0 to 21.5 per cent.

The wide differences in tariff-cutting effects of the scenarios are reflected by the differences in welfare effects, as measured in terms of overall income. The Tiered Formula scenario for agriculture excluding separate arrangements for Sensitive Products generates by far the largest increase: 74.5 billion US dollars at the world level, of which 65.6 billion US dollars are generated in developed, 8.0 billion US dollars in middle-income and 1.0 billion US dollars in low-income countries. Clearly, these outcomes result from the deep cuts made in developed countries as compared to cuts in middle-income and low-income countries.

Adding a 50 per cent proportional cut in non-agricultural products in developed countries, and 33 per cent in developing countries excluding LDCs, would generate 96.1 billion US dollars in the Tiered + NAMA scenario, of which 79.9 billion US dollars is generated in developed, 12.5 billion US dollars in middle-income and 3.6 billion US dollars in low-income countries. By far the largest part of the welfare gains is generated by the liberalization of the agricultural sector and of textiles and clothing.

In the Tiered + NAMA scenario, the largest winners among developing countries are countries in Latin America, particularly Brazil and Argentina, and some large Asian countries including China, India, Thailand and Indonesia, and the four first generation tiger economies, Hong Kong, Singapore, Korea and Taiwan. In Africa, South Africa is among the winners in this scenario. Many of these winners belong to the G-20. At the same time, some countries will experience a loss of welfare: Bangladesh, Vietnam, Mexico, some countries in Central and Eastern Europe, the Middle East and North Africa, and some countries in Sub-Saharan Africa. In this scenario, the fairly large group labelled Selected SSA is a marginal winner.

In the Sensitive + Cap scenario, however, some more Asian countries will now be among the losers, including Hong Kong and Singapore, and China, while the group of Selected Sub-Saharan countries will not experience any welfare gain at all, and the rest of Sub-Saharan Africa will be among the losers, as was the case in the previous scenario. Welfare effects for Latin America and South Africa are still positive but much smaller than in the Tiered + NAMA scenario.

So far, two main conclusions may be drawn from these results. First, the degree of ambition in terms of tariff cutting and to a lesser extent in domestic support and export subsidies, particularly in agriculture, determines to a large extent the welfare implication of the DDA. Second, welfare effects differ widely among developing countries: they are generally positive for countries in Latin America and very small or even negative for a number of countries in Asia, Africa and the Middle East.

It should be noted that concessions are made in terms of reductions in binding levels of tariffs while real welfare effects are caused by reductions in applied tariff rates. Binding levels in all WTO members are much higher than applied rates for agricultural products, and in developing countries binding rates for manufactured products exceed by far applied tariff levels. The large binding overhang requires that substantial concessions be made in order to generate meaningful real welfare effects, as observed by Joseph Francois in Chapter 4 of this volume. So far, only the proposal made by the USA has been formulated in terms of cuts in applied tariffs while all other proposals including the outcomes of the Uruguay Round dealt with binding levels.

Reforming agricultural policies

The EU and the USA

When taking into account the combined effect of the different types of protectionist measures including applied import tariff rates, domestic market support, and export subsidies, the most protected sectors are dairy products, sheep meat, beet sugar, beef and vegetable oils, while tropical products such as cane sugar, coffee and tea are much less protected. All proposals made during the negotiations so far, and all scenarios included in the study, aim at relatively large reductions of tariff rates for temperate zone products. Hence, price increases in world markets will be relatively large for such products, thus generating the largest impact on trade flows and inducing the most substantial welfare effects. In net food-exporting developing countries, this would generate large increases in producers' incomes. On top of these terms-of-trade effects generated by liberalization measures, a reduction in the use of import quotas in developed countries would reduce quota rents for exporters, particularly in sugar-exporting developing countries.

In the case of net food-importing countries in tropical zones, a price increase in international markets will reduce consumer surplus and have a negative real income effect for consumers, while at the same time the producer surplus will increase. In particular, the elimination of export subsidies in developed countries will have strong negative welfare effects on consumers in food-importing countries. These export-subsidy cuts stimulate producer surplus in exporting countries, particularly in the member countries of the Cairns Group and some members of the G-20. More specifically, elimination of subsidies on beet sugar in developed countries may create export opportunities and enlarge producer surpluses in some selected middle- and low-income countries.

From the model study by Anderson *et al.* in Chapter 2 it appears that the effects of liberalization, as generated by reforms of the agricultural sector in the European Union (EU) and the USA, are rather limited in overall size and ambiguous from the perspective of developing countries, except for the case of full liberalization. This is in part due to the combination of the general effect of liberalization and the specific effects of many different forms of preferential treatment of groups of developing countries. More specifically, the protectionist effects of the Common Agricultural Policy (CAP) of the EU, the US Farm Security and Rural Investment (FSRIA) Act of 2002, which will be in place at least until July 2006, and the previous Federal Agricultural Improvement and Reform (FAIR) Act of 1996 are reduced by preferences offered by the EU and the USA to producers in (ACP) countries, to countries included in their Generalized Systems of Preferences (GSPs), and to partners in the many PTAs.

When such arrangements are taken into account, the average weighted tariff levels of the EU and the USA are substantially lower than what appears from calculations that bypass such effects, as follows from a comparison of tariff rates by the EU and the USA in the Anderson *et al.* model using the previous GTAP5 data and the more recent version 6 of the Global Trade Analysis Project (GTAP) model. The latter model has been based on bilateral tariffs that include bilateral trade preferences and special arrangements, and many of the reforms in agricultural policies introduced since the Agreement on Agriculture (AoA) of the Uruguay Round in 1995. In countries that benefit largely from preferential access to protected markets, income and welfare of producers are supported by the relatively high prices in these export markets. This holds particularly for the markets of sugar, beef, rice and bananas. In these cases, liberalization will result in reduction of producers' income and welfare.

Some observations are in place on the direction of reforms in the agricultural regimes of the EU and the USA that have been implemented recently or are on the agenda since the AoA of the Uruguay Round. Clearly, the starting positions of countries differed widely: the sum total of domestic support and export subsidies provided by the EU in 1995 exceeded 120 billion US dollars, as compared to just over 60 billion US dollars by the USA, nearly 90 billion US dollars in the group of other protectionist countries, and less than 30 billion US dollars in the rest of the world.

The average level of bound most-favoured-nation (MFN) tariff rates in agriculture in *ad valorem* equivalents was 62 per cent after implementation of the concessions in the AoA and before the negotiations on the DDA started. Bound tariffs in South Asia and non-EU Europe exceeded 100 per cent on an average, while the average bound rates in the EU (15) and the USA were slightly above and below 30 per cent respectively (Gibson *et al.* 2001).

Since the end of the Uruguay Round, CAP reforms have been introduced to lower guaranteed prices and to decouple domestic support. Shifts in the policy regime of the USA have been quite distinct from the EU experience. It is true that initially the US regime was less protectionist and trade distorting than the EU regime was, and that the US policy stance was confrontational towards the CAP of the EU, but since the early 1990s the USA has increased domestic support with the introduction of the FAIR Act and the FSRIA Act. As compared to the previously introduced FAIR Act, which decoupled 60 per cent of US farm subsidies, the FSRIA Act relinks production and support by using target prices. Nevertheless, the EU level of support as measured by the Producer Support Estimate (PSE) – including all monetary transfers from taxpayers and consumers to agricultural producers – exceeds the support level in the USA and is above the average for all member countries of the Organisation for Economic Cooperation and Development (OECD) for nearly all commodities involved.

In the WTO, however, the USA tended to make more ambitious proposals than the EU did for liberalization of the agricultural sector on the basis of applied tariff rates and by using a harmonizing tariff cutting formula, cutting export subsidies rigorously and reducing domestic support. Potentially, the US type of proposals generate more welfare effects than the less ambitious EU proposals, which appear to be more in line with the approach followed in the AoA. At the same time, however, the more significant terms-of-trade effects of the ambitious proposals tend to have more disadvantageous welfare effects in food-importing countries.

Notwithstanding these differences in approach and ambition, both the EU and the USA seem to steer towards a further decoupling of support for the agricultural sector and consequently a reduced contribution of trade-distorting Amber Box measures, as well as a reduction of export subsidies in overall support. Moreover, for several reasons it seems likely that the PSE and the Aggregate Measure of Support (AMS), as applied by the WTO including only production and trade-distorting support, will decline in the course of time, both in absolute values and relative to the value of agriculture production at the farm gate. Some of these reasons are hardly or even not at all related to the negotiations in the WTO, but are essentially related to fiscal factors. The increasing role of Green Box measures, which are largely decoupled from production and in support of non-trade concerns in the EU, does not seem to contradict this movement, be it that it slows down a tendency to reduce the level of overall domestic support.

Developing countries

Shifting the focus now towards developing countries, we may notice that developing countries do not unanimously share a preference for substantial liberalization. The G-20 as a group has managed to play a significant role by putting substantial reform of agricultural policy on the top of the agenda. Moreover, so far the coalition has been relatively stable and robust, as emphasized by Jolanda E. Ygosse Batiisti *et al.* in Chapter 7 of this volume. The members share the vision that ambitious liberalization by developed countries is probably the most crucial component of a development-orientated outcome of the negotiations, but they seem to differ in their preference to liberalize their domestic agricultural sector. Such ambitions are high among members of the Cairns Group and among some members of the G-20, particularly in Latin America. Other members of the G-20, such as India, China and Egypt, have more modest ambitions in that regard. Many developing countries tend to emphasize Special and Differential Treatment (SDT) and the introduction of a development box. Clearly, such low ambitions regarding self-liberalization will ultimately generate more limited positive welfare effects among the countries in the South.

The implications for welfare in Africa will be among the most significant criteria to assess the outcome of the negotiations on the DDA. This holds specifically for negotiations on agriculture. Many LDCs are concentrated in this region, and large sections of the overall populations of countries in Africa are highly dependent on markets of agricultural products, both on the incomes and the expenditures side. Clearly, this holds as well for India and China. Finally, the region is highly dependent on agricultural markets for its export revenues.

The interests of African countries are not uniform and consequently their negotiation positions may differ. Some countries are highly dependent on food imports, and suffer from negative terms-of-trade effects because of increased food prices that may be due to the liberalization of world food markets. Countries may also suffer from increased import prices of food due to reductions of export subsidies in developed countries. They may also suffer loss of market shares for selected food exports because of preference erosion. These separate effects are shown by Peters and Vanzetti (2003 and 2004) on the basis of the Agricultural Trade Policy Simulation Model (ATPSM) of the United Nations Conference on Trade and Development (UNCTAD). They are addressed in a consolidated position paper of the African Union, ACP and LDC, the so-called G-90. The African Union called for a phasing-out of all export subsidies at the Kigali meeting in May 2004. In Chapter 8 of this volume, Dominique Njinkeu and Nicola Loffler are proposing a 'fast track' reduction of the AMS for those products that are of special export interests for African developing countries. If no agreement could be reached on such a proposal, African countries should be compensated in financial terms.

Although SDT for developing countries has been among the starting points of the DDA from the outset, opinions on its content differ both between developed and developing countries as well as among the countries in both groups. The principle of differentiated concessions existed already in the AoA in the Uruguay Round, including tariffication of NTBs and concessions by developed countries to reduce bound tariff rates by 36 per cent (with a minimum of 15 per cent on each tariff line); reduction of domestic support by 20 per cent; and reduction of export subsidies by 21 per cent in export volumes and by 36 per cent in expenditures, to be implemented in six years. Developing countries have committed themselves to two-thirds of these levels, to be implemented in ten years of time.

Developing countries have supported the inclusion of a development box, which would allow for lower reduction commitments concerning tariffs and domestic support measures; longer implementation periods of concessions; and expanded government assistance for agricultural and rural development, expanded access to Green Box measures, special agricultural safeguard mechanisms, preferential access to markets of high-income countries and special regulations for LDCs. If a broad concept of a development box is agreed upon, and deemed to be applicable in a wide range of developing countries including middle-income countries, prospects for expansion of South–South trade will be limited. Also, an extended version of the proposed category of Special Products for developing countries, to be exempted from tariff reduction schedules, will reduce welfare gains and specifically reduce prospects for South–South trade. Dominique Njinkeu and Nicola Loffler argue in Chapter 8 that such flexibility is likely to benefit only a limited number of African countries and products. Hence, African countries should avoid over-investing in negotiation capacity in this issue. Moreover, they focus attention on the risk that the label of Sensitive Products may cover a very large share – up to 50 per cent – of production in developed countries, including products of special interest to African countries.

If ultimately developing countries opt for seeking ambitious concessions from developed countries while aiming at reducing or postponing concessions by themselves, this constellation will limit their overall welfare gains, and favour particularly producer interests at the expense of larger welfare gains for consumers in these countries, because of the upward impact on domestic prices.

The draft Cancun text includes the proposal for full liberalization by developed countries of imports from LDCs and a specific percentage of imports from other developing countries. The Everything But Arms (EBA) initiative of the EU offers essentially tariff-free access to the EU market for products from LDCs, while free access for 50 per cent of imports from all other developing countries has been offered.

The findings by Anderson *et al.* and others lead to the conclusion that substantial cuts in applied tariff rates based on a harmonizing formula

(Swiss formula) with minimal exclusion of Sensitive Products, in combination with deep cuts in export subsidies, will contribute to welfare in most developing countries. The more emphasis is put on cuts in export subsidies and the less on tariff cuts, the smaller the group of welfare-gaining countries will be, as has also been argued by Messerlin (2004).

NAMA

The dossier of improving market access for manufactured products has attracted less attention than the agricultural negotiations, although developing countries have much to gain in this area. In Chapter 2 of this volume, Kym Anderson *et al.* show that developing countries will gain more than 7 billion US dollars in a scenario of a 50 per cent proportional cut in tariffs by developed counties, a 33 per cent cut by developing countries and zero cuts by LDCs. This result depends on the preparedness to lower high tariff rates much more than lower rates in absolute terms. This would provide an improved market access for manufactured products produced with labour-intensive technology, which dominate the manufactured export performance of most developing countries. However, many developing countries are reluctant to reciprocate by binding and lowering their own tariff rates. Given the binding overhang, the effective tariff cut will probably be relatively small, as observed by Joseph Francois in Chapter 4 of this volume.

Integrating services

International trade in services has rapidly become of significant economic interest to developed and developing countries: in both groups of countries the average share of measurable service exports in total exports was 24 per cent (in 2004), valued at about 377 billion US dollars for developing countries in 2003.

The model by Anderson *et al.* does not include the potential welfare effects of measures to liberalize international trade in services. Hence, the significance of several scenarios for service liberalization cannot be presented here in a fully integrated manner. However, liberalization effects are expected to be significant in view of the substantial share of tradeable services in the economies of many developing countries, including some LDCs. Moreover, the sectors of services and service-related FDI are often strongly interrelated with trade in manufactures and agricultural products.

As compared to all the rest of the negotiations, the negotiations on the General Agreement on Trade in Services (GATS) provide the best opportunity for a made-to-measure approach. This may be considered a 'development friendly, bottom-up approach', as Pierre Sauvé puts it in Chapter 5 of this volume, in line with a very broad interpretation of the concept of SDT. At the same time, such an approach may conflict with the overarching concept of a Doha package as a 'single undertaking'. This may be all the more serious in view of the significant size of international trade in services and its diversity. So far, the built-in flexibility in service negotiations has apparently not resulted in a strong willingness to offer substantial concessions in this area. This holds particularly for areas of special interest to developing countries, most notably Mode 4, temporary movement of service suppliers, and Mode 1, cross-border supply of outsourced services.

Realization of potential welfare gains through the liberalization of outsourcing activities under Mode 1 depends critically on the effectiveness of telecommunications services in developing countries. The quality of such services may be enhanced by FDI and increased openness in the telecommunications sector. At this point interaction is discernable between liberalization in the area of Mode 3, commercial presence or FDI in services, and the strengthening of the export potential of developing countries in Mode 1 type of services.

The economic significance of concessions by developed countries in the area of Mode 4 depends strongly on the range of service suppliers, particularly of lower-skilled suppliers eligible to enter foreign markets; on the transparency of criteria applied; on the simplicity of entry procedures; and on recognition procedures of professional qualifications. The income-generating effects of exports of Mode 4 services may be significant for developing countries, particularly in the case of countries where few alternative opportunities are domestically available for the specific skill category in case. However, Mode 4 liberalization may contribute to the brain drain and generate negative welfare effects for society at large in case it facilitates exports of skill categories that are in high demand both domestically and abroad, but are rewarded domestically at rates significantly below international levels.

More generally, in order to reap the gains from trade in services, developing countries need to implement domestic regulatory pro-poor frameworks, and need to be assisted and supported in doing so. By locking in service sector liberalization in the GATS, developing countries may strengthen their case for demanding more technical and financial assistance. Not unlikely, the closer the levels of binding are to the levels of applied regulations, the more compelling the case for external support, and the larger potential welfare gains.

Special and Differential Treatment

Developing countries have become more fully integrated in the WTO than was the case in the GATT. Not only has the number of countries involved in the negotiations increased largely, but also their mode of operation has become more substantial and consequential. Nevertheless, they still have a special position in the WTO and SDT offers them exceptions to many rules and obligations and provides them with more rights.

The traditional idea behind SDT was that trade liberalization, as practiced in the GATT and subsequently in the WTO, is not by definition promoting development. Preservation of protection of the domestic market and preferential access to markets of developed countries were thought to be powerful instruments for development. The Doha Declarations confirm the importance of SDT.

Bernard Hoekman *et al.* argue in Chapter 6 of this volume that the traditional approach to SDT 'is fundamentally flawed' and has not helped the developing countries very much. A recast of the system is required in order to make the WTO, and trade in general, more effective in promoting development. They argue that the heart of the WTO is to improve market access by reciprocity: that is where the real gains for developing countries are. Hence, improvement of market access should be realized without exceptions. However, the DWP clearly allows members to exclude Sensitive Products from the general formula and, in the case of developing countries only, Special Products, while the LDCs are completely exempted from tariff cuts in agriculture. In line with the approach of Hoekman *et al.* such exceptions should be strictly limited, not by the number of tariff lines but by a limit to the value of exempted imports, thus excluding the possibility of taking a limited number of major products out of the liberalization process, as argued by Anderson *et al.* Instead, SDT is to be realized in other ways, that is, by delinking it from continuation of protection.

Dominique Njinkeu and Nicola Loffler urge African countries to negotiate a 'fast track' to lower trade barriers for those products that are of particular interest to them. Hoekman *et al.* argue that the limitation on reciprocity offered by the Enabling Clause should be reserved to policy disciplines that are 'resource intensive to implement or that may not be development priorities for poor and small developing economies.' Tariff preferences should be reserved for the LDCs and be deep and more effective by full coverage and simplified rules of origin. There are strong arguments to reserve a more substantial role for financial and technical assistance as an instrument of SDT, as put in the next section.

The special position of developing countries was laid down in many articles of the GATT. Article XVIII, Government Assistance to Economic Development, and Part IV, Trade and Development, including Articles XXXVI to XXXVIII, added to the General Agreement in 1964, are cases in point. Part IV refers to less-developed countries as an undifferentiated group. During the Tokyo Round developing countries, as a group, aimed at negotiating SDT in the various codes that were concluded in the Tokyo Round.

The question of graduation among less-developed countries became a major issue at the Tokyo Round, and notwithstanding opposition from developing countries, the Tokyo Declaration of September 1973 refers not only to the special position of developing countries but also to the very special position of LDCs. As put in Article 6 of the Tokyo Declaration:

> The Ministers recognize that the particular situation and problems of the least developed among the developing countries shall be given special attention, and stress the need to ensure that these countries receive special treatment in the context of any general or specific measures taken in favour of the developing countries during the negotiations.

A comparable construction is included in the Marrakesh Agreement establishing the WTO, which refers to positive efforts in favour of 'developing countries, and especially the least developed among them'. Article XI, Original Membership, refers specifically to the special position of the group of LDCs recognized by the UN: these countries 'will only be required to undertake commitments and concessions to the extent consistent with their individual development, financial and trade needs or their administrative and institutional capabilities'. The Doha Declarations explicitly refer to three special requirements to support LDCs: meaningful market access, support for diversification of production and exports and Trade-Related Technical Assistance and capacity building. In that context developed countries are urged to contribute to the Integrated Framework Trust Fund and WTO extra-budgetary trust funds.

Aid for trade and development

Initiatives are required at the international and domestic level to stimulate the capacity of countries or sectors to reap the potential gains from trade, to compensate losers and to help overcome adjustment problems. Such support is not only warranted from a welfare-theoretical perspective but also from a political-economy perspective: countries that stand to lose or gain only little, may seek higher gains by obstructing such a kind of multilateral deal.

Worldwide liberalization will not only offer developing countries better access to international markets, but will result in more competition in their domestic markets as well. The inherent adjustment and restructuring costs will have to be borne by workers, public agents and private investors. To reduce the likelihood that interest groups organize an effective lobby against domestic market liberalization, social safety nets are required and visible benefits from liberalization should come to the fore in the short run.

The poor do not have much of a voice in the political arena, while they will often have much to gain from liberalization. As reflected by the positions many governments take in the negotiation process so far, the interests of producers tend to have priority over interests of consumers and the poor. The challenge for the combined trade and development community is to create synergy between trade liberalization and development cooperation in order to provide an effective stimulus for development and reduction of the number of the poor. This challenge must be addressed to finalize the negotiations on the DDA successfully, and to materialize the Millennium Development Goals (MDGs). As the Doha Declarations put it: '... trade can play a major role in the promotion of economic development and the alleviation of poverty' (Doha Declarations: Para. 2). The MDG and the Monterrey Consensus emphasize the inter-relationship between market access and terms-of-trade improvements for the poorest countries and supply-side competitiveness of these economies (UNDP 2005). To create the required synergy between trade and development cooperation, additional initiatives are required in several areas.

Trade facilitation

Tedious customs clearance, high port charges, high freight costs and slow handling add costs to traders and consequently impede trade and the exploitation of related positive welfare effects. Estimates of trading costs are rough and differ widely, and consequently expected welfare gains from reducing such costs may vary strongly. UNCTAD estimates the costs of transactions at 7 to 10 per cent of the value of trade, which could be reduced to 5 to 8 per cent by implementing trade-facilitating measures. Simple measures could reduce the costs of transactions by 2 per cent of the value of trade (Francois *et al.* 2003: Table 3.4, 32). Application of a broader definition of trade facilitation would result in higher estimates. Enhanced capacity in global trade facilitation may increase world trade by about 377 billion US dollars, the equivalent of 9.7 per cent of the value of world trade (Wilson *et al.* 2004). Improved port efficiency, service-sector infrastructure and e-business usage are among the main sources of such additional gains from trade.

Trade facilitation is included in the DDA as one of the four Singapore Issues. The special status of these four issues was related to the requirement, imposed by developing countries in the Doha Ministerial, of an explicit consensus for further negotiations to take place. This requirement was not met at the Cancun Ministerial with the exception of the issue of trade facilitation. According to the DWP, the scope of the WTO negotiations on trade facilitation will be on issues related to three GATT articles: Article V, Freedom of Transit; Article VIII, Fees and Formalities Connected with Importation and Exportation; and Article X, Publication and Administration of Trade Regulations (UN 2005: 186).

In view of the wide differences between countries in terms of their capabilities to handle trade efficiently, one may wonder to what extent developing countries will claim SDT with respect to the implementation of disciplines in these areas. Alternatively, a strategy may be pursued emphasizing the need for donor support to implement the required disciplines. Ultimately, no matter the underlying reasons, the less trade will be facilitated by developing countries, the more they will limit their own capacity to reap the gains from trade.

Trade-related capacity building

Particularly in LDCs, improved export opportunities and increased world market prices are only part of the solution (The World Bank 2005). Adequate physical infrastructure and financial services are required to exploit trade opportunities. Improving agricultural productivity requires investment in irrigation and rural electricity. To the extent that these types of facilities have the character of public goods or quasi-public goods, there is a role for governments to play in providing such facilities or in organizing the provision through public–private partnerships. Investment in productive capacity will have to be made by private persons and firms. For this, a minimum of political and macro-economic stability, and effective public services is required.

Exploiting the opportunities of liberalization of the world economy may require exporters to satisfy minimal standards set abroad or may even entail some degree of international harmonization of domestic regulatory systems. Technical standards and sanitary and phytosanitary standards (SPS) are two obvious cases in point. Meeting high levels of such standards (e.g. standards for foodstuffs) often requires large investments in testing and monitoring institutions to be paid by public means.

For that specific reason, the Technical Barriers to Trade (TBT) agreement of the Uruguay Round of the GATT refers in Article 12.7, SDT of Developing Country Members, to the need of members to 'provide technical assistance to developing country members to ensure that the preparation and application of technical regulations, standards and conformity assessment procedures do not create unnecessary obstacles to the expansion and diversification of exports from developing country members'. The Agreement on SPS of the Uruguay Round, Article 9, Technical Assistance, is even more specific in this regard, referring to both bilaterally and multilaterally supplied technical assistance in the areas of processing technologies, research and infrastructure, the establishment of national regulatory bodies, by means of advice, credits, donations and grants (GATT Secretariat 1994). The need for supporting and facilitating measures in the area of services is recognized in the GATS. According to Article IV, Increasing Participation of Developing Countries, the efficiency and competitiveness of domestic services capacity need to be strengthened through access to technology and access to distributional channels and information networks.

So far, a large part of capacity building efforts and assistance has been concentrated on assisting negotiators and policy makers in understanding the legal implications of GATS and designing negotiation positions. Pierre Sauvé argues in Chapter 5 of this volume that the focus should shift towards improving the capability to design and implement domestic reform programmes in support of a development-orientated policy regime for the service sector. More specifically, assistance may be required to support the poor in realizing potential positive welfare effects of the domestic liberalization of services. Finally, assistance may be needed to help private sector service providers to fully exploit their potential comparative advantages and take advantage of market-access opportunities.

Financial and technical support for exploiting trade opportunities

The need for donor support for trade-related capacity building was underlined in the Doha Declarations, which refer to 'the important role of sustainably financed technical assistance and capacity building programmes' (WTO 2001: Para. 41, 17–18). Three major types of Trade-Related Technical Assistance and capacity building may be differentiated. First, support for trade policy and regulation, including support for effective participation in multilateral negotiations, implementation of trade agreements, meeting technical standards and trade facilitation. Second, trade development including business development and activities improving the investment and production environment, as well as trade promotion. Third, investment in trade-related infrastructure, transport, storage, communication and energy. All three categories include activities that may be considered as public goods or quasi-public goods, and are essentially in the domain of government activities, with private–public partnerships to actually run the operation. Also, in all three categories and particularly in the second and third category, there are components where it is hard to differentiate the trade-related character from the more general character of the component.

So far, the focus on capacity building has been almost entirely on strengthening negotiation capacity and trade information capacity.

Important as these trade-related capacities may be, more capacity building efforts have to be undertaken and, indeed, to be supported externally to strengthen the capability of developing countries, and particularly LDCs, to exploit to the maximum the new trade opportunities through concessions offered in the WTO, either on an MFN basis or, for that matter, on the basis of SDT or even more favourable offers including EBA, as proposed by the EU. To exploit comparative advantages, well-functioning domestic markets and efficient transportation systems are required on top of market access abroad, market information and the capability to meet standards.

Multilateral and bilateral aid donors have made funds available to overcome all kinds of problems in exploiting trading opportunities under the title of 'Trade-Related Capacity Building' (TRCB). Early examples are the Integrated Framework that is a joint venture of the key international organizations working on trade and development and the Trade Integration Mechanism (TIM) of the IMF.

In response to the Doha Declarations, most donors increased the quantity and value of their activities in the areas of Trade-Related Technical Assistance and capacity building. This holds also for their contributions to multilateral programmes and trust funds including the Doha Development Agenda Global Trust Fund (DDAGTF). On an average, commitments to TRCB amounted to 4.8 per cent of total aid commitments in 2001–02 while 20 per cent was committed to economic infrastructure for international trade (WTO/OECD 2003; Deere 2004). The quantity falls short of the promises made in the framework of TRCB. There is also a quality problem. Aid for TRCB is delivered through a variety of channels, which entails the risk of lack of coordination. Moreover, '... assistance is rarely provided within a coherent development framework in which a trade agenda prioritizes areas of action, to improve the ability of the country to increase trade and productivity growth that provide for poverty alleviation and welfare gains' (Prowse 2002: 1248).

In this context the UN Industrial Development Organization (UNIDO) has proposed a three-pronged strategy, involving enabling developing countries to rapidly establish the essentials of a quality and conformity assessment infrastructure; to assist selective productive sectors with a high export potential to upgrade product and production quality and to establish a facility for troubleshooting and advisory service in cases where exports actually encounter technical barriers. The proposal includes setting up a trust fund.

The 2005 UNDP report on the Millennium Development Goals (UNDP 2005: 218) argues that 'there is a need to accompany global comitments to implement far-reaching trade reforms on an MFN basis with a temporary programme in order to transfer additional resources to developing countries, especially those that will experience preference erosion losses'.

Dominique Njinkeu and Nicola Loffler argue in Chapter 8 of this volume that as long as agricultural exporters in African countries suffer from protectionism and low prices, a transitional compensatory scheme should supply support to poor country producers.

Building a successful link between aid and trade is a complex and multi-layered process involving multilateral institutions, donor-recipient relations and, perhaps most importantly, domestic reforms and policies. Much energy will be required to stimulate domestic responses that enable exporters to exploit the opportunities created by multilateral trade negotiations. However, even a much-improved TRCB will not be sufficient in all cases as TRCB has only a limited impact on the institutional capability of many countries. A minimum level is needed to create an environment for investment in production capacity, which raises the question of selectivity: what is the minimum level of institutional quality that a country has to meet before TRCB and other support for trade can be sensibly supplied?

The OECD has concluded from recent experience that there is a need of: mapping and analysis of needs prior to project designing; a longer-term approach rather than short-term assistance; an integrated and comprehensive approach rather than separate projects; strong ownership; and methodological support for field offices in case of unfamiliarity with the new issues (WTO/OECD 2003: 12).

Making trade liberalization a powerful stimulus for development will require supportive initiatives in the DDA, effective support by the donor community and a supportive macro-economic framework in developing countries. In addition to the liberalization of trade in goods and services, a reformed system of SDT is necessary in order to offer a 'single undertaking' that holds sufficient promises for every WTO member. As many low-income countries will not be able to reap the benefits of trade liberalization in the short and medium term on their own, and may even incur welfare losses, technical and financial support should be made available to create an environment that turns trade opportunities into enhanced prospects for development.

Although the rationale of aid for trade as such is not questioned and donors have indicated to consider it among their priorities, some specific aspects need to be analysed thoroughly to safeguard the effectiveness and efficiency of the effort. First, when considering compensation of welfare losses due to preference erosion, an accurate assessment needs to be made of what the real meaning is of these preferences and who the beneficiaries are. Also, compensation needs to be placed in a proper timeframe. Moreover, when using the aid instrument to support the trade performance by building export-supply capacity, enhancing competitiveness and reducing the costs level of the business environment, the question has to be dealt with how to earmark funds in view of the risk of fungibility. Finally, aid for trade can only contribute to sustainable development and poverty alleviation if framed in a broader development-policy agenda.

References

Anderson, K. (2004) 'Subsidies and trade barriers', Copenhagen: Copenhagen Consensus Challenge Paper.

Deere, C. (2004) 'Capacity building and policy coherence. A role for a leaders' level G20?', Background paper for the Conference *Breaking the Deadlock in Agricultural Trade Reform and Development*, Oxford.

Francois, J., Meijl, H. van and Tongeren, F. van (2003) 'Economic benefits of the Doha Round', TD/TC/RD(2003)2, Paris: OECD.

GATT Secretariat (1994) *The Results of the Uruguay Round of Multilateral Trade Negotiations, The Legal Texts*, Geneva: GATT.

Gibson, P., Wainio, J., Whitley, D. and Bohman, M. (2001) 'Profiles of tariffs in global agricultural markets', Economic Research Service, US Department of Agriculture, Economic Report No. 796, Washington, DC: Department of Agriculture.

Messerlin, P. (2004) 'Forging a deal on agricultural trade reform', Briefing note for the Conference *Breaking the Deadlock in Agricultural Trade Reform and Development*, Oxford.

Peters, R. and Vanzetti, D. (2003) 'Making sense of agricultural trade policy reform', Proceedings of the 25th International Conference of Agricultural Economists, Durban, South Africa.

Peters, R. and Vanzetti, D. (2004) 'Conflict and convergence in agricultural trade negotiations', Geneva: UNCTAD.

Prowse, S. (2002) 'The role of international and national agencies in trade-related capacity building', *The World Economy*, 25: 1235–1261.

UNDP (2005) *Investing in Development. A Practical Plan to Achieve the Millennium Development Goals*, London: Earthscan.

UNIDO (2002) 'Feature: financing for development and trade facilitation', http://www.unido.org/doc/5106

UN Millennium Project Task Force on Trade (2005) *Trade for Development*, final report, Washington, DC: UNDP.

Wilson, J.S., Mann, C.L. and Otsuki, T. (2004) 'Assessing the potential benefit of trade facilitation: a global perspective', World Bank Policy Research Working Paper 3224, Washington, DC: The World Bank.

World Bank, The (2005) 'Realizing the development promise of trade', in *Global Monitoring Report 2005*, Washington, DC: The World Bank.

WTO (2001) *Doha Declarations*, Geneva: WTO.

WTO/OECD (2003) Second Joint WTO/OECD Report on Trade-Related Technical Assistance and Capacity Building (TRTA/CB), Geneva: WTO and Paris: OECD.

Index

For Product Safety Concerns and Information please contact our EU
representative GPSR@taylorandfrancis.com
Taylor & Francis Verlag GmbH, Kaufingerstraße 24, 80331 München, Germany